W9-ARP-756

Gareth Stevens Publishing
MILWAUKEE

About the author: Tori Derr worked in Kenya as a zookeeper at Binder Park Zoo. As a Peace Corps volunteer, she spent two years in The Gambia, West Africa. Tori now lives in Nambe, New Mexico, where she is conducting doctoral research in environmental studies.

PICTURE CREDITS
Archive Photos: 78, 80, 81
Michele Burgess: 3 (bottom), 7 (bottom), 9, 24, 48, 66, 71, 82
Camera Press: 3 (top), 13, 14, 15 (all), 45, 46, 47, 58, 59, 68, 70, 79
Camerapix: 29 (bottom), 44
Victor Englebert: 2, 6, 7 (top), 8, 16, 23 (top), 42, 63, 64
Focus Team — Italy: 4, 41, 89
Haga Library: 20, 28, 30, 65, 72
HBL Network Photo Agency: 5, 49, 55, 91
Dave G. Houser: 87
The Hutchison Library: 1, 18, 22, 25, 57
The Image Bank: 75
International Photobank: Cover, 3 (center), 21, 32, 56, 60
David Keith Jones: 50, 90
Björn Klingwall: 40
Jason Lauré: 17, 27, 29 (top), 31, 36, 37, 38, 39, 51, 73, 76, 84
North Wind Picture Archives: 77
Christine Osborne: 10, 33, 62
Chip Peterson: 34, 52, 61
Peter Sanders: 35
Liba Taylor: 19, 43, 53
Topham Picturepoint: 11, 12, 26, 54, 67, 69, 74, 85
Trip Photographic Library: 23 (bottom)
UNICEF: 83

Digital Scanning by Superskill Graphics Pte Ltd

Written by
VICTORIA DERR

Edited by
KAREN KWEK

Designed by
HASNAH MOHD ESA

Picture research by
SUSAN JANE MANUEL

First published in North America in 1999 by
Gareth Stevens Publishing
1555 North RiverCenter Drive, Suite 201
Milwaukee, Wisconsin 53212 USA

For a free color catalog describing
Gareth Stevens' list of high-quality books
and multimedia programs, call
1-800-542-2595 (USA) or
1-800-461-9120 (CANADA).
Gareth Stevens Publishing's
Fax: (414) 225-0377.

Originated and designed by
Times Books International
an imprint of Times Editions Pte Ltd
Times Centre, 1 New Industrial Road
Singapore 536196
http://www.timesone.com.sg/te

Library of Congress Cataloging-in-Publication Data
Derr, Victoria.
Kenya / by Victoria Derr.
p. cm. -- (Countries of the world)
Includes bibliographical references and index.
Summary: An overview of the African nation of Kenya that includes information on its geography, history, government, lifestyles, language, customs, and current issues.
ISBN 0-8368-2311-7 (lib. bdg.)
1. Kenya--Juvenile literature. [1. Kenya] I. Title.
II. Series: Countries of the world (Milwaukee, Wis.)
DT433.522.D47 1999
967.62--dc21 99-11355

Printed in Malaysia

1 2 3 4 5 6 7 8 9 03 02 01 00 99

Contents

PIONEER
COMMERCIAL
80

AN OVERVIEW OF KENYA

The Republic of Kenya, or *Jamhuri Ya Kenya* (JAHM-hur-i YAH KENYA) in Swahili, is a tropical country in East Africa, a region that also includes the countries of Burundi, Rwanda, Somalia, Tanzania, and Uganda. Located along the equator, Kenya supports a tremendous number of wild plants and animals. Lions, giraffes, and elephants roam its vast savannas. Snowcapped mountain peaks, sandy coastal beaches, and fascinating coral reefs make Kenya a land of great natural beauty.

Kenya's many ethnic groups share two common languages, English and Swahili. Most Kenyans live outside cities and are farmers or cattle herders, a centuries-old pattern of life in Kenya. Today, Kenyans have a blend of traditional and modern lifestyles.

Opposite: **Magnificent fiberglass "tusks" arch over Moi Avenue in Mombasa.**

Below: **Nairobi, the capital of Kenya, is a bustling hub of business and trade.**

THE FLAG OF KENYA

The current Kenyan flag is a combination of the colors and symbols of the country's leading political parties in the 1950s. It was adopted in 1963 when Kenya gained independence. The central motif of a shield and two crossed spears represents the Kenyan people's defense of freedom. Three horizontal stripes of black, red, and green make up the background of the flag. The color black represents the Kenyan people; red, their struggle for independence; and green, the country's many natural resources. The thin, white stripes between these colors represent peace and unity.

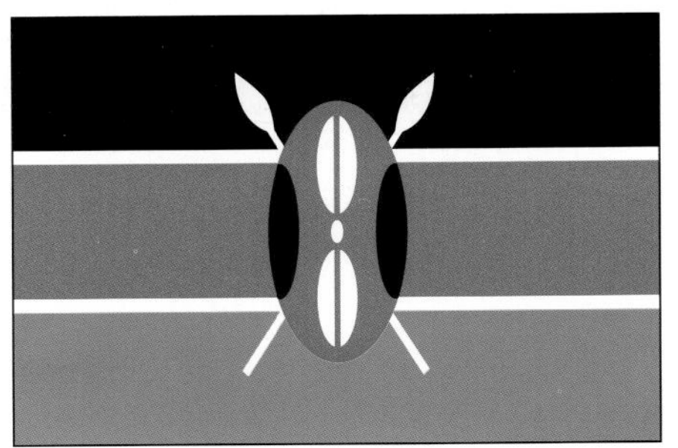

Geography

Located on the eastern part of the continent of Africa, Kenya borders the Indian Ocean and five countries: Uganda, Sudan, Ethiopia, Somalia, and Tanzania. Covering an area of 224,961 square miles (582,801 square kilometers), Kenya is slightly smaller than the state of Texas, or roughly the size of France. The capital of Kenya is Nairobi, a name derived from the Maasai name *N'erobi* (n-ay-ROB-ee), meaning "place of cold waters." Before settlement, N'erobi was a swampy area at the foot of the Kikuyu hills. Other important cities are Mombasa, on the Indian Ocean, and Kisumu, on the eastern shore of Lake Victoria. Only about 25 percent of Kenyans live in urban areas, making Kenya one of the most rural countries in the world.

Left: **The banks of the Suguta River in the Great Rift Valley are covered with salt.**

LAKE VICTORIA

The world's second-largest freshwater lake, Lake Victoria is about the size of Ireland and forms the headwaters of the Nile River. Located at the western edge of Kenya, Lake Victoria is also part of Uganda and Tanzania.

Northern Kenya and the Great Rift Valley

Dominated primarily by desert, northern Kenya is hot and arid. An area of dry, flat land, or savanna, stretches along the western part of the country.

The Great Rift Valley separates the western savanna from the rest of Kenya. Up to 56 miles (90 km) wide and 10,825 feet (3,300 meters) deep, this vast chasm stretches both north and south of Kenya's borders, from Lebanon to Mozambique. Many of Kenya's fascinating animals roam the Great Rift Valley. Beautiful lakes and extinct volcanoes line its floor. Most of the eight lakes in this valley are alkaline lakes, or *magadi* (mah-GAH-dee) in Swahili; their waters contain soluble mineral salts. The largest of these lakes, Lake Turkana, spans a distance of 160 miles (257.5 km). Among the most visited is Lake Nakuru, which supports thousands of bright pink flamingos.

TERMITE MOUNDS

Built by millions of tiny termites, these amazing structures of compacted soil can be taller than a house!
(A Closer Look, page 70)

Left: **Samburu Game Reserve is home to a variety of animals, including the African elephant.**

Central and Western Kenya

A plateau in central Kenya supports Africa's highest mountains. At 17,058 feet (5,199 m), Mt. Kenya is the highest mountain in Kenya and the second-highest on the African continent after Mt. Kilimanjaro in Tanzania. Snowmelt from Mt. Kenya feeds the Tana River, Kenya's longest and largest river, which flows east from Mt. Kenya and empties into the Indian Ocean. Hundreds of fascinating plant and animal species live in Kenya's only tropical rain forest, the Kakamega Forest in Western Province.

A Tropical Climate

Although Kenya does not have distinct summer and winter seasons, rainfall and temperatures vary dramatically between wet and dry seasons. The coastal climate is hot and humid, with monsoon winds that bring rain from the Indian Ocean. Mombasa, the major coastal town in Kenya, has an average temperature of 80° Fahrenheit (27° Centigrade).

In the northern part of Kenya, rainfall is scarce, and the climate is hot and dry. Little can grow in this region, which sometimes experiences strong winds and dust storms.

Thorny, flat-topped acacia trees dot the hot, dry expanse of southeastern Kenya, where rainfall can be as little as 6 inches (150 millimeters) per year. The Kenyan highlands are cooler than the rest of the country, and the fertile soil makes them Kenya's primary agricultural region. Few people live in the mountain ranges of central Kenya, which can get cold and wet. About 85 percent of the population lives in the southwestern region, where the climate is cooler and rainfall more plentiful than the rest of Kenya.

Below: **Acacia trees and thorny shrubs are well adapted to the hot, dry conditions of the savanna in northeastern Kenya.**

Left: Gerenuk, members of a species of antelope, frequently eat standing on their hind legs.

Wildlife Kingdom

The Kenyan savanna is covered with different varieties of grasses. Majestic baobab trees also grow in the savanna. The baobab looks as if it were planted upside down; for most of the year, its leafless branches look like roots reaching into the air. Among the most unusual of mountain plants is the giant lobelia, which grows to a height of 5 feet (1.5 m) or more and resembles a long, stalky beard. Tropical flowering plants that grow in Kenya include the hibiscus, desert rose, and morning glory.

Many fascinating animals roam the Kenyan savanna, including lions, leopards, cheetahs, rhinoceroses, giraffes, zebras, warthogs, baboons, scaly anteaters, African elephants, and hippopotamuses. Kenya's antelopes include sprightly gazelles, tiny dik-diks, and rare bongo. Wildebeests are perhaps the most numerous type of antelope; thousands of them migrate across the plains of Kenya each year. Crocodiles swim in Kenya's rivers and lakes, and the country has more than one hundred species of snakes, including the Gaboon viper and African python. Monitor lizards, which can grow to over 5 feet (1.5 m) in length, feed on young snakes and crocodiles.

SAVING KENYA'S WILDLIFE

Many of Kenya's animals are greatly prized and admired. Kenyan conservationists and scientists are trying hard to save species such as the cheetah and the black rhinoceros. These animals are threatened by disease, loss of habitat, and the illegal sale of various parts of their bodies.

(A Closer Look, page 66)

BIRDS

More than a thousand species of birds fly through or spend the winter in Kenya. Kenya's resident birds include the green ibis, white-headed wood hoopoe, hornbill, eagle, vulture, crowned crane, and kingfisher. Flamingos are a common sight on the alkaline lakes of the Great Rift Valley. Other wetland bird species include pelicans, cormorants, herons, egrets, and many kinds of storks.

History

The discovery of fossil remains in Kenya and Tanzania led anthropologists to speculate that humans originated in East Africa. Experts believe that thousands of years ago, four main groups lived in Kenya: hunters and gatherers, who roamed the plains; and three forest groups, the Cushitic, Bantu, and Nilotic people, who still populate much of Kenya today.

THE CRADLE OF HUMANKIND

Fossil finds and cave drawings near Nakuru suggest that some traditions, such as using ochre for painting and shells for decoration, have been practiced in Kenya for at least ten thousand years.
(A Closer Look, page 46)

Early Settlers and Native Tribes

The documented history of Kenya begins in about 500 B.C., when Indonesian traders brought boat-building and navigation techniques, Asian musical influence, and the coconut and banana to Kenya. Arab traders began establishing posts in coastal towns such as Mombasa, Malindi, and Lamu in about A.D. 500. Little is recorded about the activities of the native African tribes between A.D. 500 and 1500. Historians believe many of them lived as traditional farmers and nomadic cattle herders for centuries.

Below: **The ruins of Arab settlements can still be found along the Kenyan coast. Arab presence in Kenya dates back to the sixth century.**

Left: Native Kenyan chiefs pose with British officials in Mombasa. The British government set up the British East Africa Protectorate in 1895.

From the sixteenth to eighteenth centuries, many tribes fought for land, raiding one another for wealth in the form of cattle, women, and slaves. Although they could be hostile toward one another, they sometimes agreed to cooperate in times of hardship, especially drought. Trade relations between tribes strengthened during these centuries. Many of the tribes of Kenya, including the Kisii, Luhya, Luo, and Maasai, established themselves in their present-day locations at this time.

THE KENYAN COAST

Arab sailors and merchants reached the Kenyan coast in the sixth century. Over hundreds of years, the region has become a thriving, ethnically diverse trade center.

(A Closer Look, page 56)

Europeans Compete for East Africa

In the nineteenth century, Germany and Italy competed with Britain and France for colonial power throughout the world, particularly in Africa. In the mid-1800s, German and British explorers led expeditions inland to map areas of Africa previously unknown to Europeans. The British and the Germans set up trading associations in East Africa. Colonial rivalries eventually led to the division of the region into smaller political units for possession by Germany and Britain. These territories included Uganda, Tanzania, and Kenya. In 1895, the area from the coast of Kenya to the Great Rift Valley became known as the British East Africa Protectorate and was eventually expanded to the current Ugandan border. The establishment of the protectorate marked the beginning of British administration in Kenya and the rest of East Africa.

NAMING KENYA

German explorer Johann Ludvig Krapf gave Mt. Kenya its current name in the mid-nineteenth century. Krapf misheard the Kikuyu name for Mt. Kirinyaga (KER-ray-NYAH-gah) as *Kenya*. Other people attribute Mt. Kenya's name to the Maasai word *erokenya* (ARR-oh-KEN-yah), which means "snow" and refers to the white peak of the mountain. In 1920, the British East Africa Protectorate was renamed *Kenya Colony*, after Mt. Kenya.

Toward Independence

Early colonial development of East Africa was dominated by the construction of a railroad from Mombasa through vast, roadless terrain to open up communication and trade between the coast and Uganda. Settlement of the region was encouraged to support the railroad. As British and other settlers moved to Kenya, tribes living in the Kamba and Great Rift Valley were driven off their land and forced into smaller, less fertile areas and into towns. These displaced tribes included the Kikuyu, Kalenjin, Maasai, Samburu, and Turkana.

In the 1940s, Jomo Kenyatta became president of the Kenya African Union, the first legislative assembly to appoint an African leader. Faced with continued land shortages, urban unemployment, and the needs of a growing population, native Kenyans felt a growing resentment toward colonial rule and fought against the European land claims. A militant group called the Mau Mau rebelled against the British government in Kenya. Although the rebellion was put down, it demonstrated the force of Kenyan opposition to British rule, and, in 1963, the British government granted Kenya independence.

COLONIAL HEYDAY

Most European settlement of Kenya occurred after World War I in the region near Mt. Kenya, where much of the land was good for farming.

(A Closer Look, page 44)

THE MAU MAU REBELLION

Dissatisfaction among the native peoples, especially the Kikuyu, led to the organization of the Mau Mau. This militant group violently rebelled against British rule from 1952 to 1956.

(A Closer Look, page 58)

Left: **John Ndisi, Kenya's first secretary (*left*), and J. N. Karanja, high commissioner (*right*), unfurl the new Kenyan flag at Kenya House in London, England, on December 12, 1963. At midnight on the day before, the same flag was raised in Nairobi's Uhuru Stadium, ending sixty-eight years of British rule in Kenya.**

"Pulling Together"

Kenya gained independence from Britain in 1963, with Kenyatta as prime minister. In 1964, under a constitutional amendment, he became the first president of the new nation.

Kenyatta strove to involve many of Kenya's different ethnic groups in the government, promoting the concept of *harambee* (ha-rahm-BAY), Swahili for "pulling together." Kenyatta believed that unity among the different tribes was crucial to the survival and development of the new nation. During Kenyatta's rule, Kenya was among the most politically stable of African countries, preserving friendly relations with Western nations, including Britain. Kenyatta also advocated a market economy. Although Kenya's economy grew substantially under his leadership, some politicians, including former vice president Oginga Odinga of the Luo tribe, opposed Kenyatta's rule. Odinga charged that Kenyatta's capitalist economic policies served only the wealthy and neglected the needs of the rural poor. Despite Odinga's claims, however, a general improvement in living standards in Kenya ensured strong popular support for Kenyatta.

***Above:* Jomo Kenyatta's supporters, including then Vice President and Minister for Home Affairs Daniel arap Moi (*front row, third from right*), escort President Kenyatta (*pictured here on placards*) to the presidential office in 1973.**

Ethnic Struggles Continue

In 1978, Kenyatta died, and Daniel arap Moi, a member of the Kenya African National Union (KANU) became president. Although Moi initially maintained ethnic diversity within the Kenyan government, he increasingly appointed members of his own tribe, the Kalenjin, to government posts. Some junior-ranking air-force personnel and other opponents of Moi's policies tried to oust him by staging a coup d'etat, or unexpected political uprising, in 1982. The coup was unsuccessful, and ethnic problems persisted.

In the 1990s, cries for government reform increased. Odinga and others have continued to fight for a multiparty political system and for human rights for the Kenyan people. Because of increasing pressure from Kenyan groups as well as Western countries, Moi reinstated multiparty elections in 1992. According to the requirements of the Kenyan constitution, President Moi's current term will be his last in office. He will have served as president of Kenya for more than twenty years.

Below: **Daniel arap Moi reviews a guard of honor at his installation as president of Kenya in 1978.**

Jomo Kenyatta (c. 1894 – 1978)

Born Kamau wa Ngengi in 1894, Kenyatta changed his name three times before becoming Jomo Kenyatta. He learned English, mathematics, carpentry, and the teachings of the Bible from a Scottish mission in Kenya. After leaving the mission, he entered politics in Nairobi and actively campaigned to reclaim Kikuyu lands from the British. In 1963, Kenya gained independence, with Kenyatta as prime minister. The following year, he became independent Kenya's first president, an office he served until his death in 1978 at the age of eighty-four. Kenyatta is also well-known for his book *Facing Mount Kenya*, an anthropological portrait of Kikuyu life and customs.

Jomo Kenyatta

Wangari Maathai (1940 –)

The first woman in Kenya to obtain a doctorate and the first female professor at the University of Nairobi, Wangari Maathai is best known for establishing the Green Belt Movement in 1977. The movement aims to plant trees and protect the soil from erosion. It was begun to help rural women, who spend much of their time collecting firewood for cooking and heating homes. Today, more than fifty thousand Kenyan women are members, and the movement has developed more than one thousand tree nurseries and planted more than seven million trees in Kenya. Maathai has often faced resistance from some political leaders in Kenya, but support from others and from the West has allowed her to continue working for environmental protection and women's rights.

Wangari Maathai

Richard Leakey (1944 –)

The son of anthropologists Louis and Mary Leakey, Richard Leakey has made important contributions to anthropology through his discovery of more than four hundred hominid fossils in Koobi Fora, near Lake Turkana, in Kenya. Leakey's findings suggest that toolmaking ancestors of man were living in East Africa as long as three million years ago. Leakey is also actively involved in wildlife conservation and the protection of national parks. He served as director of the Kenya Wildlife Service from 1989 to 1994 and as the director of the National Museums of Kenya from 1974 to 1994.

Richard Leakey

Government and the Economy

Kenyans combine traditional with Western systems of government in making policies and decisions. After gaining independence from Britain in 1963, Kenya retained much of the colonial structure of government. The government is currently headed by the president, who is also commander-in-chief of the armed forces. The Kenyan president oversees the ministers of state, various cabinet officials, the department of defense, and the military. Popular elections are held every five years to select a president. Various ministries are responsible for making national decisions in their respective departmental domains.

NAIROBI: CITY OF CONTRASTS

Nairobi, the financial and governmental capital of Kenya, is a modern city with two faces — rich and poor.

(A Closer Look, page 60)

TRADITIONAL SYSTEMS OF AUTHORITY

Before the Europeans arrived, Kenya was not a distinct political unit but was made up of separate tracts of land governed by different tribes. Tribal authority is based on a complex system of initiation, clan and age hierarchies, and elder leaders. Today, these traditional systems continue to influence the politics of any single tribe, as well as decisions made at governmental and administrative levels.

Left: **The Kenyan parliament meets at the parliament building in Nairobi.**

Kenya is divided into eight administrative provinces. The legislative branch of the government consists of a unicameral National Assembly of two hundred members, most of whom are elected every five years. The judicial system is modeled after a combination of British common law and tribal and Islamic laws. A high court and magistrates' courts make legal decisions for the country at national and district levels, respectively. Muslims may also consult a special court on matters concerning Islamic law.

Above: **Many Kenyans participate actively in election campaigns. Political parties in Kenya today include the Kenya African National Union (KANU), the Forum for the Restoration of Democracy (FORD-Kenya), the Forum for the Restoration of Democracy (FORD-Asili), and the Democratic Party of Kenya.**

Women in Government

Kenya has a strong women's movement for equity, to improve legal rights and to increase representation by women. Although government appointments are dominated by men, women have been playing important political roles in recent years. In the 1992 election, six women were elected to parliament, and more than forty female councillors were appointed. That year also saw the appointment of Kenya's first female cabinet minister, Nyiva Mwendwa.

Fishing and Farming

About 7 percent of Kenya's land is considered suitable for farming, but only 1 percent of this is in permanent cultivation. Permanent pastures make up almost 40 percent of the land.

Nearly 80 percent of Kenyans make their living from the land by fishing, growing crops, or herding cattle. The Luo fish for tilapia and Nile perch for food, for sale in local markets around Lake Victoria, and for export to other countries. Along the coast, many people work as boat builders and menders, making ropes and sails to support maritime industries. Kisumu, Kenya's third-largest city, is a major site for fish processing and cotton manufacturing.

The fertile Kenyan highlands are good for growing crops. The Kamba, Kikuyu, Luhya, and Embu, along with many other groups, are mainly farmers. Common subsistence crops include millet, corn, beans, yams, cassavas, sugarcane, and bananas. Cash crops include tobacco, cotton, sugarcane, coffee, tea, bananas, and pyrethrum. In addition to growing crops, many farmers also raise sheep, goats, or other cattle.

TOURISM

Although most Kenyans are farmers, agriculture represents only 30 percent of Kenya's national income. Tourism and related services generate close to 60 percent of the country's gross domestic product.

Below: **Plantation workers harvest tea in the Kenyan highlands.**

Natural Resources

Kenya was one of eighteen countries to sign a Preferential Trade Area agreement for eastern and southern African states. The agreement is designed to support regional trade and cooperation in economic development throughout East Africa, a region that contains valuable natural resources, including most of the world's gold, diamonds, platinum, and manganese, as well as large quantities of coal, iron ore, natural gas, and other minerals. Among Kenya's own natural resources are gold, limestone, rubies, garnets, and soda ash.

SAFARI!

Encounters with Kenya's splendid wildlife await visitors to the country's fifty or so national parks and reserves.

(A Closer Look, page 64)

Left: **Factory workers manufacture bead jewelry for export. To combat Kenya's rapidly growing rate of unemployment, estimated at 35 percent in urban areas in 1994, the government has looked for ways to increase industry through the production of consumer goods, including furniture, textiles, soap, and flour.**

Imports and Exports

Kenya imports mainly consumer and capital goods. The country also produces some of its own consumer goods. Since independence, Kenya has relied on a few major exports: coffee, tea, pyrethrum, sisal, and products from oil refining. In the 1990s, however, Kenya expanded its markets by developing new product areas, recognizing that a diversity of exports could help stabilize the economy when individual markets fluctuate. Horticultural crops have become increasingly important to Kenya's economy in recent years. In 1998, Kenya was among the world's largest exporters not only of tea and coffee, but also of flowering plants. Most exports are shipped to European, African, and Middle Eastern countries.

ELEPHANTS AND THE IVORY TRADE

Kenyans are among the strongest opponents of the infamous ivory trade. A ban on the export of ivory and ivory products has helped put the country's ailing elephant population on the road to recovery.

(A Closer Look, page 48)

People and Lifestyle

Numbering more than forty, Kenya's ethnic groups belong to three major language families: Bantu, Cushite, and Nilote. The Bantu people came to Kenya in the first millennium, bringing with them knowledge of blacksmithing and agriculture and displacing the hunters and gatherers who were living in Kenya at that time. The Kikuyu, Luhya, Kamba, Kisii, and Meru are all Bantu people. The Nilotic people consist of the Maasai, Turkana, Samburu, Kalenjin, and Luo. The Cushitic people include the Somali, Boran, Rendille, and Oromo. They are thought to have originated in Ethiopia and other countries north of Kenya.

ETHNIC COMPOSITION

The five largest tribes in Kenya are the Kikuyu, Luhya, Luo, Kalenjin, and Kamba. Minority populations of Arabs, Indians, and Europeans have also settled in Kenya.

The Kikuyu

The Kikuyu settled in the Kenyan highlands during the seventeenth century. Traditionally farmers, they are also skilled weavers and blacksmiths. They were among the first East African tribes to establish relations with European settlers and to become Western educated.

Below: **Most rural Kikuyu are farmers who grow bananas, sugarcane, yams, millet, beans, and corn. The tribe was one of the first to adopt Western dress.**

Left: **Maasai women wear necklaces and bracelets consisting of many strands of small, brightly colored beads.**

HEALTH IN KENYA

Kenya's national health problems include malnutrition, malaria, and AIDS. The government and many Christian health organizations are working to improve sanitation, education, and health care in the country.

(A Closer Look, page 54)

The Swahili

The Swahili are a Bantu group. Today, many of them have Arabic ancestry. They traditionally make a living from fishing and agriculture. They are also skilled in wood carving, weaving, and metalwork. Swahili is Kenya's national language.

The Maasai

Although they represent only about 2 percent of the total population of Kenya, the Maasai are among Kenya's best-known and most photographed tribes. Of mixed Nilotic and Cushitic ancestry, they share many Nilotic customs, including the shaving of heads, the extraction of two middle teeth from the lower jaw, and a single-legged, storklike stance. Like the Turkana and Samburu people, the Maasai are nomadic cattle herders who live mainly on a diet of cow's milk mixed with blood. During the nineteenth century, the Maasai were greatly feared for their raids on other tribes.

Although all Nilotic people were originally cattle herders, many Luo became farmers and fishermen after settling along the eastern coast of Lake Victoria hundreds of years ago.

NOMADIC PEOPLES

The Maasai, Turkana, Samburu, and Somali people are primarily nomadic or seminomadic cattle herders, using camels to transport goods as they follow their herds in search of pastures.

(A Closer Look, page 62)

Above: **The family is the basic unit around which Kikuyu life is structured.**

Clans and Kinship

Family is an integral part of social life in Africa. Although there are many unique practices among the different ethnic groups of Kenya, many customs are also shared. Most ethnic groups have similar initiation ceremonies, marriage customs, and social organization patterns centered around the family unit.

Kikuyu life is organized around the immediate family. Several families together form a homestead. Several homesteads make up a larger subgroup, and many subgroups make up a clan. There are altogether nine clans in the Kikuyu tribe. Elders make important decisions at clan meetings. Among the Kisii, clans are identified by animal totems, such as a leopard or zebra. The Maasai and Samburu hold ceremonies to initiate young boys into warriors. Samburu warriors are allowed to marry about five years after their initiation.

Family Legacy in a Name

Many tribes have ceremonies for naming newborn children. The Kamba believe that naming children after their grandparents is a way of continuing their family life cycle. The first son is named after the paternal grandfather and the second son after the maternal grandfather. Similarly, the first daughter is named after the paternal grandmother, and the second daughter after the maternal grandmother.

Above: A Samburu woman weaves plants into the roof of her family's hut.

Women

Many tribes in Kenya, including the Kisii and the Samburu, initiate girls into womanhood through circumcision. In most agricultural communities, women are responsible for gathering wood and carrying water, as well as for cultivating crops. Their social lives frequently center around their shared activities and the raising of children.

Urban Families

City dwellers of Arab and Asian ancestry do not identify with the clan associations of Kenyan tribes. Clans and heritage continue to be very important to the identity of city-dwelling tribal Kenyans, who retain an awareness of their links to rural or tribal areas where their relatives might still live. Westernized families, however, favor Western lifestyles, and do not always rely on kinship structures as much as rural Kenyans.

Left: Well-to-do families in Nairobi enjoy modern comforts. Urban Kenyans tend to blend traditional with Western lifestyles.

THE WOMEN OF KENYA

Women play a vital role in the development of Kenya, in domestic as well as professional settings.
(A Closer Look, page 72)

Formal Education

European missionaries set up the first schools in Kenya in the late nineteenth century. Education remained the responsibility of Christian missions until after World War II, when the colonial government, along with Kenyan participation, founded various universities, including the Royal Technical College of East Africa, founded in Nairobi in 1954.

Today, the national education system consists of three levels: eight years of primary education, four years of secondary education, and four years of university education. Although Kenyan history, language, and culture are part of the curriculum, education remains largely modeled after the British system. English is the dominant medium of instruction, and students are expected to achieve proficiency in subjects such as mathematics, English literature, and history. Young Kenyans also take a keen interest in sports, especially soccer and rugby.

Although many children complete primary and secondary education in Kenya, it is much more difficult for Kenyan students to receive a university education. Graduating high school

TRADITIONAL LEARNING

Before the colonial period in Kenya, children were educated by their extended families, clan elders, and through initiation ceremonies. The history of one's family and tribe were passed down in stories and oral histories, and important moral lessons were frequently taught through proverbs.

Below: **Kenyan children are educated in English.**

Above: **A Kenyan teacher conducts adult literacy classes outdoors.**

students must take an entrance examination to qualify for admission to one of Kenya's four public universities. Only about 2 percent of those who complete high school qualify. An even smaller number can afford the higher tuition fees of private universities. For the same reasons, few Kenyans have the opportunity to study at overseas universities. They must have great drive and ambition to attend a university. Some work for years to earn enough money for a university education.

Achievements in Education

Following independence, the government worked to increase the numbers of primary and secondary schools in the country. Today, there are also many more teacher-training institutions, technical and trade schools, and universities in Kenya.

The Kenyan people's strong commitment to education has paid off. Today, Kenya has one of the higher literacy rates in Africa — about 80 percent of Kenyans can read and write English or Swahili. Much work remains to be done, however, in providing education and promoting its importance, especially among women in rural communities.

GOING TO SCHOOL

Although an average of four out of five Kenyans are literate, education does not reach many people, especially girls, in rural areas. In some districts, the literacy rate can be as low as 30 percent.

(A Closer Look, page 52)

Left: **Many Luo are Christians. Christianity is Kenya's main religion. About 40 percent of all Kenyans belong to various Protestant denominations, and 30 percent belong to the Roman Catholic Church.**

Christianity and Other Beliefs

Kenya has no state religion. The majority of Kenyans today are Christians, largely due to the efforts of European missionaries in the nineteenth and twentieth centuries.

Although many Kenyans practice an introduced religion, such as Christianity or, to a lesser extent, Islam, they retain many of their tribal beliefs, including creation myths. According to Kikuyu legend, Gikuyu, the founder of the tribe, was guided to Mt. Kenya by *Ngai* (en-GAI), the Kikuyu's divine spirit. Gikuyu and his wife settled on Mt. Kenya and had nine daughters, who began the nine principle clans of the Kikuyu.

The Kamba, too, recognize a single god, Ngai, believed to live in heaven or, occasionally, on high mountains or in trees. The Kamba only call on Ngai in times of great community need, such as when rain does not fall and crops are dying. At these times, the Kamba offer sacrifices to Ngai for help.

The Kikuyu and Kamba believe in ancestor spirits. Like the tradition of naming children after their grandparents, ancestor

JOK

Unlike the Kamba and Kikuyu, who are both Bantu groups, some of the Nilotic people do not believe in a central deity but in several "chiefdom deities," collectively called *Jok*.

spirits reflect the continuation of a life cycle. Ancestors, also called the "living dead," are frequently contacted and given food and drink. Neglecting ancestors can result in harm to living family members. The Kamba and Kikuyu also have special medicine men who prescribe herbs and use magic to cure illnesses.

Maasai and Samburu Beliefs

The Maasai believe in one supreme being, also called Ngai, who created the universe. Unlike the Kamba, the Maasai do not believe in a continuation of life spirits after death except for the *oloiboni* (ol-oi-BON-ee), or ritual leader. When an oloiboni dies, he is buried in a hole. It is believed that the soul of an oloiboni will be reborn as a snake. Maasai therefore do not usually kill snakes. The Samburu also believe in Ngai. They revere the highest point in the Samburu district, Mt. Ng'iro, as a special holy place of Ngai. The majority of Maasai and Samburu have adhered to their tribal religious beliefs, and only a small percentage has converted to Christianity.

Below: **Muslims on the island of Lamu celebrate Prophet Muhammad's birthday with a ritual mock fight. Many of Kenya's coastal communities are Muslim.**

Language and Literature

The national language of Kenya is Swahili, a member of the Bantu branch of languages. Swahili has been influenced by Arabic, and, to a lesser extent, Portuguese and other languages used by traders and sailors who arrived in Kenya.

The earliest forms of Swahili derived from Arabic script in the early eighteenth century. Swahili was used extensively along the coast and functioned, during the colonial era, as a shared language among the British East African colonies of Kenya, Tanzania, and Uganda.

Swahili is easy to read, but many of its sounds are quite different from English. For example, in Swahili, the letters *n* and *g* commonly occur together at the beginning of words, for example, in *Ngai*, the Kikuyu divine spirit. People greet each other in Swahili with *jambo* (JAHM-bo), which means "hello," and thank each other with *asante* (ah-SAN-tay). In addition to English and Swahili, many Kenyans speak the languages of their ethnic groups.

Left: A sign in the Nairobi Arboretum Forest Reserve states the rules of the reserve in English (*left*), Swahili (*center*), and Arabic. While the national language, Swahili, unites Kenya's diverse ethnic groups, the country's official language is English.

Literature in Swahili and English

Most Swahili literature consists of stories that were originally handed down in an oral tradition. Today, many have been written in Swahili and English.

Contemporary Swahili writings include traditional tales, romance novels, and mysteries, as well as novels that depict the political and social struggles of the 1950s and 1960s. The historical novel *Uhuru wa Watumwa*, or *Freedom for the Slaves*, written by James Mbotel in the 1930s, is an important Swahili work. Contemporary Kenyan novelists writing in Swahili include Ali Jemaadar Amir and Katama Mkangi.

Ngugi wa Thiong'o, or James Ngugi, was born in Limuru, Kenya, in 1938. He was the first East African writer to complete a novel in English. *Weep Not, Child* (1964) portrays a Kikuyu family during Kenya's struggle for independence. Other novels by Ngugi include *The River Between* (1965), *A Grain of Wheat* (1967), and *Petals of Blood* (1977). Ngugi's work addresses the political, social, and cultural struggles of the Kenyan people and has earned him a reputation as an important social critic.

Above: **Residents of Nairobi enjoy reading in Uhuru Park, a center for cultural activities and events.**

Below: **Kenyan writer Ngugi wa Thiong'o is known for his powerful novels.**

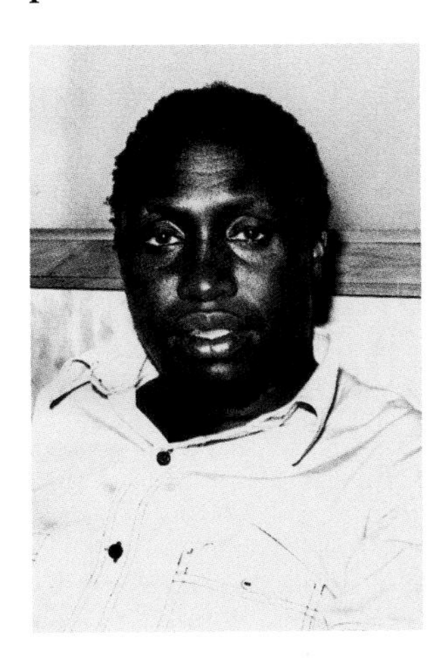

Arts

Traditionally, artisans in Kenya made ordinary objects such as spoons, spears, or baskets for use at home and work. They worked to please tribal leaders or gods, and their incentives came from spiritual hope and praise from their community. Today, tribal artisans still duplicate patterns and pass on techniques across generations, thus perpetuating their artistic culture. Some patterns have symbolic meanings or depict important scenes in the group's history.

Crafts

Many artisans decorate practical and household items. The long gourds used by the Maasai to hold milk are usually decorated with colorful beads. The Swahili are skilled in woodworking and weaving. They make beautifully carved doors, including the

Below: **Maasai paintings use dyes from the earth. White and yellow dyes come from clays, and a red ochre is obtained by mixing clay with the juice of wild nightshade.**

Above: **Woodcarving is a fairly lucrative trade in Kenya. Carvings of Kenyan wildlife are frequently exported to countries in Europe and North America.**

intricate work on the doors in Lamu. They also weave coconut fibers into household items. The Kamba are skilled craftspeople responsible for many wood carvings of Kenyan wildlife. They weave the fibers of baobab and fig trees into baskets.

Soapstone Art

Soapstone is a rosy-white stone that comes from quarries in western Kenya, where the Kisii live. The Kisii are well known for their soapstone carvings and for the "Kisii stool," a low seat elaborately covered with colorful, beaded patterns. Although soapstone was originally used for practical items such as bowls and pipes, Kisii carvings are now quite commonly sold in North America as decorative home items, such as candlesticks and vases. Among the well-known subjects in soapstone sculpture are a mother and her child and the "thinker," a man in a contemplative pose. Together, they represent the importance of family, kinship, and reflection to the Kisii. Soapstone is also applied in a powder form to the face for ceremonies, such as circumcisions and funerals.

Above: **Kikuyu dancers perform in traditional dress and body paint.**

Dances

Kenyan tribes dance for a particular purpose, usually a ceremony or event, rather than solely for entertainment. Most Kenyan dances are accompanied by drums or other instruments, such as flutes and shakers. The Kikuyu, however, have traditionally danced to singing, with no other musical accompaniment.

Dances performed by Kikuyu children and adolescents tend to prepare them for initiation. For example, older children teach younger children the *rukiu* (ROO-kee-oo), a basic dance that includes steps and rhythms useful for later dances. As children grow up, they progress through many other types of dances. Kikuyu warriors and maidens have about seven different dances. In order to earn the right to participate in these dances, the warriors and maidens must first pass through their initial novice dances and receive permission of the elders. The *mugoiyo* (MOOG-oi-yoh) dance occurs after the long rains are over and when most crops are close to maturing. The mugoiyo is always

SOUNDS AND RHYTHMS

From tribal drumming to the complex rhythms of the Kenyan *rumba* (room-BAH), music brings people together and enlivens parties and festive occasions in Kenya.

(A Closer Look, page 68)

danced at night by the light of a special fire made by women. In all Kikuyu dances, women choose their dance partners, and men have no say in the matter.

Coastal Architecture

Homes and building styles vary markedly throughout Kenya. Coastal towns are characterized by a mixture of Arab architectural styles and unique building materials. Many buildings in Lamu and Mombasa are constructed of coral. Soft coral is used for various carved decorative pieces on buildings, and harder coral is used for foundations, walls, and roofs. Poles made from mangrove wood are also used for construction. Many doors, especially in Lamu, are carved with intricate floral and geometric patterns and stylized leaves.

In many Swahili towns, homes are built close together, connecting families and neighbors and creating alley-like streets that provide space for people to interact freely. Open squares near the waterfront were traditionally reserved for boat repair.

Below: A mosque in Lamu boasts intricate architectural details, such as decorative railings and window screens.

Leisure and Festivals

Most Kenyans must work hard to earn a living, either through farming and herding or through the development of small businesses in a sometimes struggling economy. Leisure is a rare pleasure for many citizens, but whenever they have the time to relax, Kenyans enjoy themselves wholeheartedly.

In the countryside, many people build social interaction and games into their work. For example, many women enjoy cooking or washing clothes together so they can chat and share news of their families and community. The Embu sing as they work and have songs on just about every topic for just about every occasion — for cultivation, millet threshing, cattle herding, beekeeping, and beer making. Young Samburu children often like to wrestle and to carve toy bows, arrows, and spears out of wood.

Left: *Kigogo* (ki-GO-go) is a simple, popular game that involves moving counters around a board to capture the opponent's pieces.

Unwinding in Urban Kenya

Cities such as Nairobi and Mombasa afford many opportunities for leisure activities. In Nairobi, people go to theaters, discos, museums, art galleries, and the movies. An international center, Nairobi has many local clubs. It hosts events featuring music and culture from around the world, including Indian film and Latin

American and Caribbean dance. Movies and plays are heavily influenced by American, European, and Indian styles, although film festivals sometimes focus on local cultural issues. Galleries in Nairobi display the diverse talents of the Kenyan people, and, during the day, the market places in Nairobi are a hub of activity for native Kenyans and tourists alike.

Chai

Many Kenyans have afternoon tea, or *chai* (CHAY-ee) in Swahili, at about 4 p.m. Kenyans generally take their chai with milk and sugar. Meeting for chai is an important opportunity to spend time with family and friends and to catch up on the day's events. Kenyans also enjoy talking about local and world politics over chai.

Left: **Among the Swahili in Lamu, the launch of a new boat is a communal activity that usually takes place on a Friday afternoon. After praying in the mosque, people gather to push the boat into the water, chanting in unison as it is launched.**

Above: **Training, discipline, and natural speed and agility rank Kenyans among the best track athletes in the world.**

Leaders of the Pack

Kenya has some of the fastest long-distance runners in the world. Since 1964, the country has won thirty-two Olympic medals, including twelve gold. Kenyan men are also consistent winners of the Boston and New York marathons in the United States. In 1996, Kenyan athletes won six of the top ten places in the New York City Marathon.

While Kenyan men have been given the opportunity to compete in marathons throughout the world, Kenyan women have not received as much sponsorship. They are talented runners, but the traditional roles of women in Kenyan society have led many to quit running at the peak of their careers in order to marry and raise a family.

The Kenya Amateur Athletics Association has been striving to provide more opportunities and sponsorship to women runners and to help them succeed at the Olympic Games, where, despite the triumphs of male Kenyan runners, Kenyan women have not yet received a medal. Kenyan women have done well in other cross-country races, however, including the Boston Marathon, the New York Marathon, and the World Cross Country Championships.

Soccer

One of Kenya's most popular sports is soccer. Fans come from all walks of life, and amateur games are enjoyed in parks and stadiums every weekend. Kenya's national team, the Harambee Stars, competes regularly in the World Cup and other international matches. Other teams compete in regional and continental tournaments.

Other Sports

Although skiing is not a typical sport in Kenya, the country sent its first national cross-country skier to participate in the Winter Olympic Games in Nagano, Japan, in 1998. Philip Boit, who originally trained as a distance runner, learned to ski only in 1996.

Car racing has become a popular activity in recent years, with international events such as the Rhino Charge, held in Nanyuki, and the annual Safari Rally. Kenyans also enjoy cricket and wrestling. In resort areas and cities, golf and boat racing are popular.

Below: **Players and spectators alike are enthusiastic about soccer.**

Rites of Passage

Circumcision marks the transformation of a boy into a man. Ceremonies can proceed for many days or weeks and are an important time for boys in the same age group, called a set, to bond and move forward to new roles in society.

Among the Samburu, a new age set is initiated when eight boys, representing the eight Samburu clans, are selected to be circumcised on Mt. Ng'iro, a holy mountain for the Samburu. These eight boys will become the leaders of their age set. About a year following this initiation ceremony, preparations for a mass circumcision, called *lorora* (lor-OR-a), begin. Boys wear capes of blackened goatskin to announce the beginning of their transition to manhood and roam between different homesteads, singing special songs. They are led by older initiated men to traditional places where they will gather wood and gum (a sticky substance

***Below:* A Samburu woman shaves her son's head in preparation for circumcision.**

Above: **Kenyans stand as President Moi enters Nairobi's Nyayo Stadium at the start of Kenyatta Day celebrations.**

from certain plants) for bows, arrows, and clubs. Several days or weeks later, each boy's mother shaves his head before circumcision and prepares a special bed for resting after the ceremony.

Samburu boys appoint two men to hold their legs and shoulders during circumcision. These men are regarded as godfathers for the rest of their lives. The actual circumcision is very quick, and boys are courageous, showing little sign of pain or fear. Circumcised boys are then decorated with copper wire earrings and a special headdress of black ostrich feathers on a band of braided palm leaves.

After circumcision, boys prepare themselves for the ceremonies of being a *moran* (mor-AHN), or warrior. There are five such ceremonies, and the last can occur as many as five or more years after circumcision. These ceremonies mark a period of transition, when newly initiated men learn the skills of warriors.

National Holidays

On December 12, Kenyans celebrate Jamhuri, or Independence Day, with parades. Many city dwellers head to the countryside to spend the holiday with their relatives and friends. Another national occasion is Kenyatta Day. Celebrated on October 20, it marks the anniversary of Jomo Kenyatta's arrest in 1953 by the British for his alleged involvement in the Mau Mau Rebellion.

GETTING MARRIED

Tribal marriage customs in Kenya usually involve gifts of cattle or goods and elaborate rituals. Western-style wedding ceremonies are popular in the cities.

(A Closer Look, page 50)

Food

Although many urban Kenyans cook in modern kitchens with gas stoves, most rural women cook over an open fire. For them, in addition to tending and harvesting crops and preparing meals, the daily cooking chores include collecting firewood. Many rural women thus devote most of their time to feeding their families.

Most Kenyan dishes are made by combining grains or starchy foods, such as yams, potatoes, or plantains, with meat or a sauce. They are served on a large platter or bowl. Everyone eats together from the same dish. One of the most popular Kenyan foods is *ugali* (OO-gahl-ee), a cornmeal porridge made by mixing cornmeal with cold water and a little salt. The mixture is added to boiling water and stirred until it sets into a semisolid. Ugali is served with vegetables or, on special occasions and if the family can afford it, chunks of meat. Other Kenyan dishes include chicken and coconut milk mixed with many spices and served with rice; a spicy bean and coconut-milk stew served with rice or

FRUIT

Tropical fruit is an important part of the Kenyan diet. Bananas are used for food and for making beer. Monkey bread, the fruit of the baobab tree, is used to make cool drinks. Monkey bread, which has a bittersweet taste, is also eaten as a snack.

***Left:* A Maasai woman cooks ugali.**

Above: **Fresh fruit and vegetables are sold in open markets throughout Kenya.**

porridge; and baked curried fish. Kenyan meals also feature a lot of green vegetables, including kale, collard greens, and potato leaves. Sauces prepared from these vegetables are served with rice or meat. Many dishes in Kenya have been influenced by Asians, who brought spices and different ways of preparing foods to Kenya many years ago. Chicken tikka and vegetable curry came from India, and the coconut and its uses came from Indonesia.

The Kenyan Diet

Urban Kenyans cook or buy food from supermarkets, just as in other countries. In rural Kenya, farmers grow a wide range of food crops, including millet, sorghum, cassavas, yams, corn, potatoes, beans, and pumpkins. Many families also raise goats and sheep for meat. The primary food for many nomadic people is milk, either fresh or curdled, and sometimes mixed with blood from cattle. The Maasai are forbidden to eat most kinds of meat, although some eat sheep, goat, eland, or buffalo. Milk, sometimes served with millet, constitutes about 80 percent of the Turkana people's diet.

A CLOSER LOOK AT KENYA

Kenya boasts an incredibly diverse geography and culture. This section provides an insight into important aspects, past and present, of the country.

Early Kenyan history may well hold the key to the mystery of human origin. Evidence pieced together from fossils suggests that ancestors of modern human beings roamed parts of Kenya hundreds of thousands, perhaps even millions, of years ago.

Opposite: **Elaborate bead headbands, earrings, and necklaces are part of the Samburu traditional dress.**

Above: **Polo and other sports, such as cricket, were introduced to Kenya by the British.**

Modern Kenya has been shaped by a variety of influences. From the tenth to the nineteenth century, nations battled to control the country's coastal regions. The British arrived in the 1800s, and safaris attracted European hunters and settlers to Kenya in its early colonial days. Kenyans have shown their courage and strength throughout these difficult periods of change. The Mau Mau, a militant nationalist group, fought against British rule from 1952 to 1956. The British granted Kenya independence in 1963. Despite setbacks and unequal treatment in the past, the women of Kenya have made significant contributions to the country's development. Today, many Kenyans strive to protect their wildlife heritage, but conservation efforts are not easily reconciled with the nomadic lifestyle of some ethnic groups.

Colonial Heyday

Long before the British conceived of a railway across East Africa in the late nineteenth century, the Kamba people had already predicted the arrival of "strangers" and the "long snake," or railroad system. They knew change was coming. The construction of the railroad marked the beginning of the colonial era in East Africa. Without the railroad, or "Lunatic Line," as it was called, there might have been no coffee or tea plantations, no Indian traders, no British colony. The British brought close to twenty thousand Indian workers to East Africa to build the 600-mile (965-km) railroad, intended to transport goods between Uganda and the Kenyan coast. Building the railroad proved a costly enterprise. Even the returns from materials as valuable as ivory were not enough to cover the expense of its construction.

The outbreak of World War I in 1914 disrupted European settlement of Kenya. British and German settlers abandoned their farms to fight in German East Africa, today's Tanzania. After the war, some settlers returned to their farms, while others decided to

THE "WHITE HIGHLANDS"

From 1903 onward, the British government provided inexpensive leases to Europeans interested in investing in "unoccupied" lands. In fact, many native Kenyans were forced off land that their tribes had occupied for generations. This land was then used to cultivate large-scale export crops such as coffee and tea. European settlement in Kenya was concentrated in the fertile highlands, which became known as the "White Highlands."

develop hunting safaris, which brought more Europeans to East Africa. These elaborate safaris often lasted weeks at a time. Europeans were guided through the savanna with a troupe of porters and servants, who aided in the hunting of big game.

Above: **Many white settlers remained in Kenya after independence in 1963 and made the country their home. Some of their children learned African languages before they learned English. Today, white Kenyans participate actively in all sectors of Kenyan life.**

Opposite: **Maasai senior chief Lenana poses with white officials who moved his tribe off traditional Maasai grazing land.**

Living in Kenya

Despite the glamorous image of hunting safaris, colonial life in Kenya was not easy or leisurely. European farmers struggled with learning to farm in a foreign land. Large tracts of forest had to be cleared to plant coffee or tea, and plantations were often larger than a single family could manage, even with the hiring of Kenyan workers. Newly planted crops were threatened by floods, locusts, and, sometimes, waterbuck or other game. The failure of plantations led some settlers to turn to mining. Gold mining became profitable in the 1930s, but mostly on a small scale for individual families. Gold helped some settlers make it through the worldwide economic recession of the 1930s. After Kenya gained independence in 1963, many Europeans chose to remain in their new home.

The Cradle of Humankind

Paleontologists, or scientists who study fossilized animals and plants, believe early humans may have originated in parts of East Africa, including Kenya. Two famous scientists, Louis and Mary Leakey, made many important discoveries in Olduvai Gorge, in Tanzania. In 1959, Mary Leakey unearthed the fossil of a hominid, a two-legged mammal of the same family as modern humans. She and Louis named it *Zinjanthropus*, now regarded as a member of the genus *Australopithecus* and believed to have lived more than 1.75 million years ago. In their long careers, the Leakeys discovered three kinds of hominids: *Homo habilis*, *Homo erectus*, and *Australopithecus*.

Kenyan Richard Leakey, son of Louis and Mary, made further contributions to the study of human origins. His best-known discovery was in the Koobi Fora region of eastern Lake Turkana, in Kenya, close to the Ethiopian border. Richard Leakey found a skull similar to that discovered in the Olduvai Gorge by his parents, only this skull was believed to be at least 2.6 million years old.

Left: **Louis Leakey (*second from left*) shows visitors to the King George V Memorial Museum in Nairobi the *Zinjanthropus* skull he and his wife, Mary, discovered in Olduvai Gorge in 1959.**

Left: **Richard Leakey holds in his right hand the skull of *Australopithecus* and in his left his groundbreaking discovery — the skull of a hominid at least 2.6 million years old. Leakey's find proved paleontologists' theories that at least two kinds of early humans coexisted.**

Uncovering an Ancient Past

Richard Leakey and his team of researchers set about finding fossils in Koobi Fora through a process called surface prospecting, which involves searching for areas in the fossil beds where teeth and bones are exposed. When a fossil is found, a geologist identifies its stratigraphic level, or position in the rock layers, which helps determine the age of the fossil. These fossils are extremely fragile, and the experts exercise great care in removing them from the surrounding rock, using special dental picks and camel-hair brushes. After fossil pieces are recovered, they are usually reassembled in a laboratory or museum.

Leakey's finds shed light on how our human ancestors lived between 10,000 and 400,000 years ago. We now know that they used red ocher clay in their hair (a custom still practiced by some African tribes, including the Maasai). They also used shells and ostrich egg beads for adornment.

Lake Turkana yielded the fossils of nearly a hundred mammal species, most of which are now extinct. By studying the rock layers of the region, Leakey has learned how Lake Turkana might have looked more than one million years ago. He believes that what is now a dry, barren land was once wet forest, and that prehistoric animals, such as three-toed horses and saber-toothed tigers, roamed the land.

Elephants and the Ivory Trade

The African elephant is the largest mammal on land, weighing one to two tons. A baby elephant takes twenty-two months to mature in its mother's womb and can weigh 200–265 pounds (90–120 kilograms) at birth. The large ears of the African elephant help cool its large body, and its tusks are used for fighting, digging, and eating. Its long, flexible trunk is used for breathing, feeding, and drinking, as well as for touching and gesturing to other elephants. An elephant can drink 50 gallons (189 liters) of water a day.

Below: **Rangers protect elephants in reserves, and guides ensure that visitors do not harm these magnificent animals. Tourism dollars that come from elephant watching have been estimated at U.S. $25 million per year.**

Elephants have long been admired for their splendid ivory tusks. Prized in Europe, Asia, and North America, ivory has been profitably traded for hundreds of years. In parts of Asia, elephant tusks are ground into a powder and sold as an aphrodisiac. Hard and durable, ivory is also a popular material for carving. Piano keys were formerly coated with ivory; this is the origin of the phrase *tickling the ivories,* meaning "playing the piano."

Endangered by the loss of natural habitat and the ivory trade, in which elephants are killed to "harvest" their tusks, the elephant population in Kenya has been dwindling since the 1970s. Of the 130,000 elephants that once roamed the Kenyan savanna, only 20,000 now survive. In an effort to save the elephant from extinction, in the 1980s, a ban was placed on any trade of ivory. The ban was imposed on all nations under the Convention on International Trade in Endangered Species (CITES). Richard Leakey was a key figure in enforcing the ban of ivory trade in Kenya. After the ban, the price of 2.2 pounds (1 kg) of ivory plunged from $300 to $30, and the elephant population began to recover. Although elephants are still considered threatened today, their numbers have been on the rise in recent years.

Left: An ivory carver shows off his elephant carvings. Although we are not sure about this particular carver, and despite a strict ban on the ivory trade, many ivory carvers continue their practice. Carved ivory pieces fetch high prices in Europe and North America.

Getting Married

Many tribes in Africa practice polygamy, meaning that each man is allowed to have more than one wife. Today, however, polygamy is practiced mainly in rural areas and is dying out in the cities.

Most African tribes have intricate courtship and marriage customs. These include presenting the family of the bride with some form of payment, called bride wealth, often cattle. In other tribes, the custom is reversed; the bride presents the groom's family with a dowry, also frequently cattle. These exchanges of cattle or goods serve to formalize the marriage.

For many Kenyans, marriage is a means of accumulating wealth from repeated gifts of dowry. Girls usually marry between the ages of thirteen to eighteen, depending on their tribes. Many urban women, however, marry later, preferring to complete their education first. Men generally marry between the ages of sixteen and twenty. In many tribes, men and women cannot marry until they have completed their initiation and circumcision ceremonies; only then are they considered adults.

Left: **A Samburu bride and groom (*far right*) bless goats during their marriage ceremony. In many tribes, especially nomadic groups, cattle represent wealth. Camels and goats are bestowed as gifts, loans, and dowry or bride wealth.**

Left: A Catholic priest solemnizes a Western-style wedding in Nairobi.

The Kisii Way

The traditional Kisii custom involves a bride wealth payment to the intended bride's family. When a Kisii couple decides to marry, the man's father asks a friend or relative to negotiate a bride wealth payment satisfactory to both families. After the groom's father delivers the agreed number of cattle to the bride's family, an *egekobo* (EY-gay-ko-bo), or "escort," ceremony can be arranged. Egekobo involves the bride and groom spending alternate days in each other's homes to ease the bride into separation from her parents' home. These occasions are usually accompanied by delicious meals, which are believed to facilitate the transfer of fertility to the groom's home. Fertility is especially important to the Kisii, who believe it is a tragedy to die without having any children.

Changing Customs

Many traditional African practices common before the colonial era have been affected by urbanization, Westernization, and increased conversion to Christianity. City dwellers tend to favor modern ceremonies. In recent years, Kenya has seen an increase in church and secular weddings more consistent with Western than with traditional African culture.

THE LUO WAY

In a traditional Luo wedding ceremony, the bride's grandmother places an animal skin in front of the groom's mother's house. The bride and groom stand on the skin while the bride's grandmother covers them with a special butter. A vine is placed around the bride's neck. After this ritual is performed, the guests celebrate with a wedding feast at the home of the bride's parents.

Going to School

In the nineteenth century, British missionaries established schools in East Africa, especially in Uganda and Kenya. Many mission schools taught children to read and write English so they could read and understand the Bible. Most education in primary or secondary schools was not based on African history but on British and European literature, history, and culture. Today, the Kenyan education system remains modeled after the British. Although the number of schools increases throughout the country every year, and Kenya has an 80 percent literacy rate, the country still faces problems in making education available to all sectors of its population.

Women's Education

In many African countries, the formal education of girls and women is often neglected or consists only of primary school education. Many poor, large families cannot afford to send all their children to school. Girls frequently remain at home, helping their mothers with household chores and looking after their siblings. This is especially true in the rural areas of Kenya. Social

Left: **These Kenyan girls are walking to school. The enrollment of girls in Kenyan schools is much lower than that of boys.**

Above: **Many Kenyan women learn to read and write relatively late in life, in adult literacy classes.**

customs in many parts of Kenya also dictate that women marry at a very young age. Approximately 20 percent of mothers in the Mandera district in northern Kenya are adolescents. The responsibilities of marital life and motherhood disrupt women's education. In the Lamu district, for instance, two out of every five girls quit school before completing their secondary education.

Rural Education

School attendance and literacy rates are much lower in rural areas than in cities. In the Kisumu district, for example, 30 to 40 percent of women cannot read and write. Adult literacy programs that impart basic skills to help Kenyans run their farms and businesses are a relatively recent development. Because children in nomadic tribes are needed to tend cattle, they are especially unlikely to receive more than rudimentary education unless they abandon their traditional way of life.

Despite these struggles, the government continues to support and promote education. There is also growing recognition among the people that education is a chance to expand children's minds and equip them to move away from poverty.

Health in Kenya

Health care in Africa is generally poor. Although the projected life expectancy for a Kenyan at birth is high for Africa, it is only fifty-five years. Child malnutrition, malaria, and Acquired Immune Deficiency Syndrome (AIDS) are among the chronic health problems that plague the country.

Malnutrition

Women have special health needs, especially related to their role in childbearing and rearing. Undernourished mothers often experience complications in giving birth and breastfeeding. Their newborn babies risk being underweight and physically stunted.

Left: **A Kenya Christian Council worker feeds a young famine victim. More than one-quarter of Kenyan children are born moderately to severely underweight. Many do not live beyond the age of five. These problems stem in part from widespread poverty. Many Kenyans depend on cattle or crops for food and income; in a drought, people are unable to afford health care. Many Kenyans also do not have access to health care facilities, immunization clinics, or safe drinking water.**

Left: **Kenyans wait in line at a clinic just outside of Nairobi. Most existing health care facilities are small and run by Christian churches. In the Turkana district in northern Kenya, more than 75 percent of health clinics are run by the Catholic Church.**

AIDS: Killer Disease

About two-thirds of the world population infected with the human immunodeficiency virus (HIV) that leads to AIDS live in sub-Saharan African countries, such as Kenya, where the fertility rate is high, and health education services are poor. The majority of newly infected people in East Africa are young, between the ages of fifteen and twenty-four. Women are particularly vulnerable because of the young age at which they tend to marry and because many marriages are polygamous, with men having more than one wife, enabling the disease to spread quickly.

Educational programs have helped slow the rate of infection, but many adults are resistant to educating youth about HIV and AIDS, fearing that open discussion of sex-related issues will encourage an increase in sexual activity. Every year, death from AIDS results in many children being ophaned, and some households must now be run by grandparents or elder children. Extended family support programs have been successful in helping Kenyan families affected by HIV/AIDS. A United Nations organization called UNAIDS is working to combat the spread of the AIDS virus in Kenya and sub-Saharan Africa, and some countries have succeeded in stabilizing or lowering the rate of infection.

The Kenyan Coast

Arabs were among the first foreigners to arrive in Kenya. From the tenth to sixteenth centuries, many Arabs sailed to the coast of Kenya in boats called *dhows*. For many centuries, Arabs and coastal people traded African gold, ivory, and slaves for beads, cloth, and metal tools from India and Arabia. Arab explorers and traders were instrumental in the establishment of important trading towns such as Mombasa, Lamu, Malindi, and Zanzibar. The Arabs influenced the development of these towns and the culture through the construction of narrow streets and buildings that resembled their own settlements in the Middle East, and in bringing Islam to Kenya. Arabic forms of architecture remain in these cities today. Arabs also intermarried with many of the Kenyans living along the coast, especially the Swahili, and were a dominant influence on culture and language in Kenya for many centuries. Only from the fifteenth century onward did European countries become interested in trade along the Kenyan coast.

CULTURAL INFLUENCES

Over its long history, the Kenyan coast has seen Persian, Chinese, Malayan, Portuguese, and British influence. Traders from many different cultures passed through coastal Kenya on their trade routes between Europe and East Asia via India. The Portuguese brought many crop plants, including corn, cassavas, cashews, tomatoes, and tobacco, to Kenya.

Below: Mombasa is an active center for trade in the Indian Ocean.

The coast is lined with beautiful sandy beaches, mangrove trees, and coral reefs. Fishermen use poles made from mangrove wood to propel their boats through the water. Mangrove wood is also a common building and export material. Formed over hundreds of years by millions of tiny coral polyps, coral reefs support large populations of fish, crabs, starfish, and shrimp. Visitors flock to the coast to admire its stunning array of marine life. Scuba diving has become a popular tourist activity, and marine parks have developed along the coast to support the growing tourism industry. Coral is used to build many of the houses along the coast, and the roofs of these houses are made from coconut leaves.

SLAVERY

In the eighteenth century, the French and Arabs participated in slave trading. Africans were brought to the Kenyan coast and sold as slaves. The French sent them to India, and the Arabs sent them to their plantations in Zanzibar, Pemba, and other places. Slavery was not abolished until 1897, after the British took control of the coast.

Left: Dhows, or Arab boats, travel along the East African coast, from Somalia to Zanzibar, Tanzania.

Coastal Communities

Today, the Kenyan coast is a melting pot of people and cultures. Although people of African ancestry make up the majority of the coastal population, many people of Asian descent settled in Mombasa and other port towns in the mid-eighteenth century. Arabs, too, have had a long history of occupation along the coast. A diversity of religious beliefs is evident in the many mosques, churches, and Hindu temples located in coastal towns and cities. In Lamu, the Bajuni people and coastal Bantu live alongside Arabs, Somalis, and Indians.

The Mau Mau Rebellion

The Mau Mau was a militant nationalist movement organized in the 1950s, primarily by people of the Kikuyu tribe. Led by Dedan Kimathi, whom some have described as a rebel and a fanatic, the Mau Mau opposed British rule, especially policies that gave British settlers the rights to land traditionally belonging to the Kikuyu.

Before the arrival of European settlers from the late nineteenth century onward, most Kikuyu lived in the highlands surrounding Mt. Kenya. In the late 1930s, the British ruled that no person of African or Asian descent could own land in the area. White settlers seized some of the best agricultural land belonging to about one million Kikuyu people. The Kikuyu were relocated to small, less fertile reserves. Many of the farms the colonists established were too big for them to manage, so Kikuyu squatters were allowed to live on parcels of farmland in return for labor or rent.

Left: **British-led troops comb the forests for members of the Mau Mau movement in the 1950s.**

Left: **Handcuffed to a British guard, Waruhio, one of the leaders of the Mau Mau movement, is led to the courtroom for his trial. Waruhio's original death sentence was changed to life imprisonment when he offered to arrange the surrender of other leaders of the movement.**

Dissatisfied with the land laws that the British had established, Kenyans began forming political organizations in the 1920s and 1930s. Jomo Kenyatta and the Kenya African Union (KAU) were successful in settling some four thousand land claims for the Kikuyu, but the land they received had formerly belonged to the Maasai and was not particularly suitable for farming.

Political tensions increased, and the Mau Mau Rebellion broke out in 1952. Kimathi led group members to the forests of Mt. Kenya, and they frequently raided farms and homes for food. People did not feel safe in their homes, and they enclosed their villages in fencing. The British declared a state of emergency in October, 1952, and arrested Kenyatta the following year for his alleged association with the uprising. The British fought the rebels and interrogated people suspected of cooperating with the Mau Mau. By the time the rebellion was suppressed in 1956, about 13,000 Africans had been killed and more than 100,000 Kikuyu forced to relocate to dry land and detention camps. An estimated 30 to 100 British died. Although the rebels were defeated, their actions demonstrated Kenyans' strong nationalist feelings. Independence was eventually granted in 1963.

Nairobi: City of Contrasts

At the beginning of the twentieth century, Nairobi was little more than a swampy valley where the Maasai took their cattle to graze and drink. Conveniently located at the midpoint of the railway from Mombasa to Uganda, the city of Nairobi was established in the late nineteenth century. The railroad brought traders, travelers, and settlers to Nairobi. As the settlement developed, hotels, houses, and clubs were built. Today, many of these historic buildings remain. Towering office and apartment buildings have also taken shape in this modern city.

Below: **Nairobi has a population of more than one million people. Although many ethnic groups used to reside in particular neighborhoods, these distinctions have blurred in recent years, making Nairobi a melting pot of cultures.**

Nairobi is the financial and governmental capital of Kenya, the hub of tourism and business, and the site of many excellent African history, art, and natural history museums. The city is also home to Kenya's small tire, beer, chocolate, and textiles industries. Although Nairobi has several large shopping malls and markets, most shops are small *duka* (DOO-kah) run by Indian or Pakistani families who have settled in Nairobi.

Most Nairobi residents live outside the bustling downtown area. Some own beautiful mansions, relics from the colonial period and from the post-independence growth of the city. Nairobi's growing middle class lives in apartments and houses. Despite the wealth of some urban sectors, Nairobi is plagued with high unemployment. Many homeless families live in makeshift shacks of cardboard or corrugated metal. These families have among the worst living conditions in Kenya, often lacking adequate water, sanitation, food, or shelter. An estimated 2.5 million people live in slum areas as squatters and make what living they can from running small, streetside huts selling metal boxes or charcoal-burning stoves. The dual nature of Nairobi — the colonial alongside the modern, luxury alongside poverty — makes it truly a city of startling contrasts.

Left: **In the poorer parts of Nairobi, women display fruit and vegetables for sale along the streets.**

MARKETS

There are more than ten major markets in central Nairobi. These include the City Market, in the heart of Nairobi; the Kariokor and Wakulima Markets, primarily meat and farmers' markets; and the Gikomba Market, which stretches along the Nairobi River and sells beautiful cotton cloth, scrap metal, curios, and crafts. Outdoor markets are popular because their goods are much cheaper than those in fancier city shops.

Nomadic Peoples

Following seasonal patterns of rainfall, Kenya's nomadic tribes herd their cattle over vast tracts of land in search of fresh pasture. Daily life centers around the herd and involves protecting it from thieves or predators. Family wealth is measured by the number of cattle owned. Nomadic peoples in Kenya include the Maasai, who reside mostly in the south of Kenya, and the Turkana and Samburu, who live mainly in the northern region. All three ethnic groups speak Nilote languages, and the Samburu and Maasai speak the same language, Maa.

The Maasai

The Maasai believe that if a person cares for his or her cattle, the person and the community will prosper. As part of their initiation into adulthood, young Maasai men are sent to the bush with only a spear to kill a lion. This task cultivates the warrior skills needed to protect their cattle. Many Maasai used to believe

Below: **The traditional dress of a Maasai moran includes bead necklaces and plug earrings, as well as ostrich feathers, helmets of lion mane, and monkey-skin anklets. Maasai shields and spears are decorated with dyes from the earth.**

Left: Turkana nomads lead their cattle to water holes in a dry riverbed near Lake Turkana.

that all cattle once belonged to them and that they had a right, therefore, to take cattle from other ethnic groups. Up to the early twentieth century, the Maasai engaged in cattle raids throughout Kenya.

Before the colonial era, the Maasai roamed an area of approximately 1,500 square miles (3,885 square km) in both Kenya and Tanzania. Colonial settlement and policies relocated many native Kenyans, especially the Maasai, to reserves, where they suffered because their herds had to compete with wild animals for pasture. Today, nomadic groups face an uphill struggle to survive as cattle herders. Many Maasai have abandoned their nomadic lifestyle for farming in southern Kenya.

WARRIORS AND LEADERS

Maasai warriors live in a *manyatta* (mahn-YAH-tah), a separate housing settlement consisting of about fifty huts shared among Maasai of the same age set. Once a leader is chosen, he will lead his age set into old age.

The Samburu and Turkana

The Samburu people have traditionally been more peaceful and tolerant of other ethnic groups than the Maasai. Samburu respect is given to everyone, especially to the person who owns the most cattle. Like the Maasai, the Turkana have also faced daunting changes in their livelihood, and many have adapted to agricultural and urban occupations.

Safari!

The Swahili word for "journey," *safari* (sah-far-EE), conjures up images of African wildlife in all its splendor. During Kenya's colonial period, big-game hunting safaris became very popular among Europeans. Today, safaris are usually for photographing animals only; killing protected animals is prohibited. Every year, organized tours bring thousands of tourists to Kenya's national parks to see their famous wildlife. The country has developed an extensive national park system.

The first national park in Kenya, Nairobi National Park, was established in 1946. Two years later, Tsavo National Park was set up. Covering an area of more than 8,000 square miles (20,720 square km), the park is divided into two areas, Tsavo East and Tsavo West. Tsavo West is home to the largest elephant population in Kenya. These elephants roam not far from the Mzima Springs, which are fed by underground waters of volcanic origin. The springs support many crocodiles, and underground viewing areas put visitors at eye level with hippopotamuses treading slowly across the riverbed.

***Below:* Zebras gather at a water hole in Tsavo West Game Reserve.**

Above: **Better roads and facilities have increased the number of tourists in Kenya in recent years and given visitors better access to parks and reserves. The most popular of the fifty or so national parks in Kenya are in the southern part of the country.**

The Maasai Mara Reserve is located in the Serengeti plains, which extend into Tanzania. The dry savannas of Maasai Mara support many migratory animals, including wildebeests and zebras. Many tourists take hot air balloon rides over the Serengeti, where the sheer vastness of the land is breathtaking. The Samburu National Reserve is located in the heartland of the Samburu people. Home to a number of unique species found only in northern Kenya, the park's animals include Grevy's zebras, Somali ostriches, and Beisa oryx. Spectacular Marsabit National Park, much less visited than some of the parks farther south in Kenya, is located on a volcano. The forested mountain region forms a refreshing oasis in an otherwise stark desert.

Responsible tourism has become the focus of many who recognize the need for tourist dollars in Kenya's economy and the simultaneous need to strike a balance between tourism and its potentially negative effects both on wildlife and on the people who live near parks. One-quarter of every dollar earned goes toward the establishment of health care facilities and schools for the human communities surrounding the parks. For Kenyans, tourism represents at once a chance to make money and a lost opportunity — the inability to use safari land and its resources for other purposes.

Saving Kenya's Wildlife

The African elephant and black rhinoceros have become endangered because of trade in animal parts, such as tusks and horns. Other animals in Kenya are also threatened by human presence and diseases introduced by new crops.

The Fastest Animal on Land

Capable of a running speed of 70 miles (113 km) per hour, the cheetah can overtake a car. It relies on its extraordinary speed to hunt down fast-moving creatures, such as small antelopes and hares, that other predators cannot catch. Much of the savanna on which cheetahs live has been converted into farmland. Trading in spotted furs has been prohibited since 1975, but illegal hunting continues to diminish the cheetah population.

Left: **Tourists on safari eagerly photograph a cheetah. Most safari animals have become so accustomed to humans that they wander right up to jeeps and vans.**

Left: **Conservationists are fighting to save the black rhinoceros from extinction. Hunted for the high price its horn brings on the black market, this gentle giant is disappearing faster than any other large animal on Earth.**

The Black Rhinoceros

The word *rhinoceros* means "horn nosed" in Greek. The horns protect the animal against predators and aid in territorial fights with other rhinoceros bulls. The rhinoceros also uses them to dig for minerals that supplement its diet.

In some Middle Eastern countries, rhinoceros horn is made into knife handles. In Asia, people value the horn for its alleged medicinal properties. Rhinoceros horn is worth more than gold in many Asian markets — a pound of horn fetched $2,300 in Taiwan the late 1990s.

In fact, rhinoceros "horn" consists of densely packed hair, not ivory. It is not a true horn, and most experts believe it has no medicinal properties at all. In recent years, many Asian countries have banned the import and sale of rhinoceros horns. Conservationists hope to save the rhinoceros by making the live animals' contribution to tourism more valuable than returns from the sale of their horns and other parts.

Sounds and Rhythms

Like many aspects of Kenyan culture today, Kenyan music is a blend of African, European, Asian, and American styles. In particular, music from the Democratic Republic of the Congo (Zaire) has influenced some Kenyan musical forms, including the *rumba* (room-BAH). Zairean music and the rumba share intricate rhythms and are popular for dancing.

Other musical styles in Kenya are derived from the traditional Kikuyu, Luo, Kamba, Luhya, and Swahili music. Kamba and Kikuyu music are popular in the cities and are characterized by their fast rhythms. Although the *benga* (BAIN-gah) style originally belonged to the Luo people, the Kikuyu and Kamba have also popularized it. A style common among some Luhya is *omutibo* (om-ut-EE-bo), which combines guitar music with tapping on soda bottles. Along the coast in Mombasa and Lamu, a popular Swahili style of music called *tarabu* (tahr-ah-BOO) is played at weddings and on other festive occasions.

Left: **Music and musical performances are important features of Kenyan culture. These boys' musical instruments are known as melodicas.**

Left: **Dancers of the Maragoli tribe in Kisumu whirl to the pounding rhythm of drums.**

The only way to really understand Kenyan music is to hear it. Best-selling Kenyan compact discs include *Benga Blast!* by Daniel Owino Misiani and the Shirati Band, and *Ashara,* by the popular Saifee Band.

Drums, Bells, Shakers, and Strings

Traditional musical styles are popular in Nairobi as well as rural areas. The Luhya practice a traditional drumming style called *isukhuti* (EE-soo-koo-tee). Many drums are made from hollowed wood or from tin, with animal skin stretched over the top. Certain drumbeats were, at one time, played to communicate with other members of the same tribe across long distances.

Other traditional instruments include leg bells, shakers, and fiddles. The Boran, Embu, Kikuyu, Luo, and Maasai tribes wear leg bells. These are usually animal skins filled with peas or beans. They are played by tying them to the legs and stamping the feet. Shakers resemble tambourines and are made by stringing shells, bottle caps, or small pieces of tin on a wire. Many tribes, including the Luhya, Luo, Kamba, and Kikuyu, also make string instruments. Both traditional and contemporary music play important parts in Kenyan culture and grace many special occasions, including wedding and circumcision ceremonies.

Termite Mounds

Termites are insects that feed on grass and dead trees. Like ants, termites are social insects with a complex system of interaction. Many kinds of termites build huge, underground homes. Others build hard mounds of soil that rise high above the ground, and some build their nests in trees. Termite mounds are a common sight on Kenyan savannas. Some can be as enormous as 25 feet (8 m) high and 36 feet (11 m) wide! Termite colonies consist of a maze of interconnected cells, resembling those in a beehive or ant colony. These cells often contain fungi that the termites eat. The fungi in termite mounds are also part of some Africans' diets.

Left: **Some termite mounds dwarf even the Maasai, who are known for their height.**

Left: **Antelopes are among the many animals that rest or play on termite mounds.**

Termites play an important role in the ecosystem by decomposing plants and returning their nutrients to the soil. About one-third of all dead plants are broken down and consumed by termites. Termite mounds can improve the fertility of soil and create flood-proof spaces where trees and shrubs are better able to grow. Termites can, however, also be serious agricultural and forest pests. They damage cotton, sugar, and tea plants, and their mounds make plowing difficult. Termites can cause damage by eating the wood, mud, and grasses that are used to build many Kenyan homes. Cleaning a rural African home includes knocking down termite nests from the roof beams and walls.

Dens for Other Animals

Hyenas, bat-eared foxes, and jackals sometimes make their homes in abandoned underground termite nests. These dens protect the animals against predators and shelter them from the scorching sun. Other animals occasionally rest or play on abandoned termite mounds. When lionesses hunt, they sometimes leave their cubs among termite mounds, which conceal the cubs from predators. The tunnels and channels of the mounds make good playing spaces for the cubs. Learning to maneuver on mound slopes improves their hunting skills.

The Women of Kenya

Until recently, many Kenyan women were excluded from education and had no legal rights to land. Today, however, they are forging careers in urban sectors. Whether their lifestyles are traditional or contemporary, women are important contributors to the development of Kenya.

Traditional Roles

Women's literacy rates in rural areas lag behind men's. In some districts, up to 40 percent of women cannot read or write. Some of this inequality is a relic of the colonial era, when men were encouraged to receive an education and work for the British, while women remained traditional homemakers. Men still tend to move to urban areas to find work to support their families in the countryside. Apart from inheriting property when they marry, most women do not have legal access to land.

Women are primarily responsible for the cultivation of crops for consumption in Kenya, looking after more than 70 percent of

Below: **Women sell fruits, vegetables, grains, and prepared foods in open markets on the outskirts of Nairobi.**

Left: **Members of the Green Belt Movement begun by Wangari Maathai carry seedlings that symbolize their aim of preserving Kenya's natural resources.**

Kenyan crops. Many married women decide which crops to grow and how to manage the land. They select seeds, plant and harvest crops, and process the crops for meals, storage, or sale.

Tackling Urban Problems

Not all women's programs are held in rural areas. Throughout the country, adult literacy programs for women have helped women establish themselves in nontraditional, career roles. Women's programs have also been instrumental in lifting urban families out of poverty. Many of Nairobi's poorest families, called urban peasants, live without land to farm, scraping together a living out of virtually nothing. An estimated 150,000 children grow up on the streets of Nairobi without access to adequate food, shelter, clothing, or education. Street children reflect the huge social repercussions of modern Africa's economic trials. This sad picture is a stark contrast to that of the traditional African family, where the child is the heart of household and nation. As the Kenyan government looks for ways to solve these problems, Kenyan women are playing a crucial role in developing urban craft or trade projects. Income from these efforts allows families to buy land or rent homes as a first step toward a hopeful future in the city.

WORKING FOR THE COMMUNITY

Kenyan women tend to be socially active, organizing small groups to improve farming practices and to develop small-scale projects to raise money for their families. Women also attend classes in adult literacy, nutrition, family planning, or first aid. They fund these and other special projects with beekeeping or the sale of handicrafts, such as pottery, baskets, or beadwork. Money from these projects is also used to improve sanitation and nutrition, and to build schools, health clinics, and community centers.

RELATIONS WITH NORTH AMERICA

North American involvement in Kenya began in the early twentieth century, when North American missions played an important part in developing schools and health care facilities in Kenya. East African safaris also attracted many North Americans to Kenya. Political relations between Kenya and North America remained limited, however, until the late 1950s, when African representatives sought support from other countries in gaining independence from Britain. When the United Nations passed the Declaration of the Granting of Independence to Colonial Countries and Peoples in the 1960s, it was strongly backed by then U.S. President John F. Kennedy. This declaration helped speed up Kenya's independence, originally targeted by Britain for the 1970s.

In the post-independence period, North American involvement in assistance to Kenya increased. In the 1960s, the United States donated money to help the Kisii develop a carving partners cooperative. Today, aid from North America supports economic and small business developments in Kenya.

***Opposite* and *below*:** **Tourism contributes significantly to Kenya's national income.**

Christian Missions

Today, many North Americans work and live in Kenya, a large number as Christian missionaries. Missions to Kenya began in the nineteenth century and were fundamental in the development of the country's first schools and in the conversion of Kenyans to Christianity, the dominant religion today. North Americans in Kenya are also active in the running of health care facilities, schools, and humanitarian projects. Many were involved in relief efforts after the bombing of the U.S. embassy in Kenya in 1998, helping to provide money, counseling, and temporary shelter to victims of the blast.

Roosevelt in Kenya

During his administration, U.S. President Theodore Roosevelt established 125 million acres (50 million hectares) of national forest, doubled the number of national parks, and created sixteen national monuments and fifty-one wildlife sanctuaries in the United States.

In 1909, just after completing his last term in office, Roosevelt went to Kenya on a hunting and collecting expedition. The trip was sponsored by the Smithsonian Institution, which was interested in collecting plants and animals from East Africa for scientific study. Roosevelt and his team of biologists collected

Left: Missionaries and priests from all over Kenya gather at a stadium during the 1985 visit of Pope John Paul II. North Americans were among the missionaries who brought Christianity to Kenya in the nineteenth century and helped develop the country.

Left: **Roosevelt's contributions to wildlife study remain controversial today. Although his animal specimens helped scientists learn more about many species, the cruelty of his hunts earned him the nickname "Bloody Teddy."**

more than 14,000 specimens of plants and animals, from small creatures, such as rodents, to some of Kenya's most majestic animals, such as the rhinoceros and the African elephant.

Following his trip to Kenya, Roosevelt wrote *African Game Trails*, a book describing his expedition and the Kenyan lands of the early twentieth century. Coverage of his expedition in American newspapers and periodicals popularized big-game hunting as a sport in East Africa. Some experts have suggested that national parks in Kenya were modeled after the U.S. national park system, which Roosevelt helped develop. More recently, however, animal conservationists have charged that Roosevelt's hunts were cruel. Although, in part, he collected animals to better understand them, some conservationists nicknamed him "Bloody Teddy," because he killed more than five hundred buffalo, elephants, rhinoceroses, leopards, and cheetahs. Thus, Roosevelt left an important, if debatable, legacy on Kenyan lands.

Political Tensions and Clashes

By the 1990s, Kenya's economy, once among the strongest in sub-Saharan Africa, had deteriorated due in part to government mismanagement. Important international aid donors such as the World Bank withheld financial assistance from Kenya in the early 1990s in response to President Moi's resistance to constitutional reform. The United States increased pressure on Moi to allow multiparty elections and to improve human rights and economic conditions in Kenya. Many Kenyans were dissatisfied with the power of the central government, and ethnic tensions in western Kenya and Rift Valley Province drew international attention.

By the 1997 election, President Moi had allowed revisions to the constitution, including multiparty elections. Despite these changes, many still felt the election, which resulted in the reappointment of President Moi, was unfair. Violent outbreaks following the election resulted in more than a hundred deaths in Rift Valley Province. The United States threatened Moi with sanctions and limitations to political rights in an effort to curb further violence. According to the Kenyan constitution, a new president must replace Moi in the next election, in 2002.

Above: **University students stand up to Kenyan police, who surrounded and closed the university in Nairobi in July, 1997. Widespread rioting followed the reappointment of Daniel arap Moi as president in 1997.**

Bombing of the U.S. Embassy in Nairobi

On August 7, 1998, a car bomb exploded at the U.S. embassy in Nairobi, killing twelve American citizens and more than two hundred and fifty Kenyans and injuring close to five thousand people. The bombing was allegedly a terrorist act led by Saudi Arabian militant Usama bin Ladin. Another terrorist bombing occurred almost simultaneously at the U.S. embassy in Dar es Salaam, Tanzania. In retaliation for these attacks and to prevent other terrorist acts believed planned for U.S. embassies around the world, the United States launched missiles at a terrorist training base in Afghanistan and a chemical plant in Sudan allegedly involved in the production of chemical weapons. Both facilities were associated with bin Ladin.

The U.S. government pledged substantial aid toward rebuilding the three-block-radius business district in Nairobi ruined by the bombing. To strengthen trade relations, the United States also agreed to increase the number of American trade specialists in East Africa and to add two American citizens to the Kenyan commerce staff.

Below: Scores of relief agencies offered assistance in response to the terrorist bombings in 1998. Canadian, U.S., and U.N. development agencies provided medical supplies, search-and-rescue equipment and workers, and counseling support.

Current Relations

Former President Jomo Kenyatta worked hard to establish warm relations with neighboring countries, Europe, and North America. Relations between North America and Kenya have generally been friendly since the colonial period, allowing continued and successful North American involvement with development projects, health, and conservation efforts.

In the 1980s, however, differences arose over elephant and other endangered species trade agreements. The ban imposed by CITES on ivory has remained a source of controversy and tension between African nations and the United States.

In the late 1990s, groups in the United States lobbied for the exclusion of Kenyan runners from U.S. marathons, claiming that Kenyans dominate the races and that their exclusion would make the top places in marathons more accessible to American citizens. This view was strongly opposed by many Kenyans and Americans who feel that Kenyans have every right to participate in U.S. races and that these runners have been an inspiration to athletes in Kenya and throughout the world.

Below: **Kenyan President Daniel arap Moi met with U.S. President Bill Clinton at the opening of the Entebbe Summit for Peace and Prosperity on March 25, 1998, in Uganda.**

Left: **Kenyan Moses Tanui (*front*) and his countryman Lameck Aguta (*second*) lead competitors past the 12-mile (19.3 km) mark in the 1997 Boston Marathon. Aguta went on to win the race.**

Kenyans in North America

Kenyans come to America for many reasons. Many Kenyan athletes have spent time training in the United States. Other Kenyans come to pursue academic, musical, or business careers. Famous Kenyan writer Ngugi wa Thiong'o served as a visiting professor of English at Northwestern University in Illinois.

Some Kenyans have immigrated to the United States and Canada to sell the handicrafts and artwork of their people, and, like millions of other immigrants to America from around the world, some come simply to pursue education or a more prosperous life. North American universities offer opportunities to receive an excellent education. Many Kenyan students fortunate enough to study in North America return to Kenya to work. Some, however, find jobs in North America, then send money home to their families.

Above: **American tourists visit a Samburu village.**

North Americans in Kenya

Kenya's national parks and vibrant cities draw hundreds of North American tourists to the country each year. Tourism has opened up most of Kenya, and although many tribes and villagers still have traditional lifestyles, they are familiar with Western customs, and many have learned English.

The Peace Corps

Established in 1961, the Peace Corps is a U.S. governmental agency of volunteers working in countries all over the world to improve education, health, agriculture, trade, and business. Peace Corps volunteers have been working in Kenya since 1965, filling jobs designated by the Kenyan government as special areas of need. Part of their job includes learning the culture of the host country and sharing their own culture with Kenyans. Education volunteers usually teach mathematics, physics, chemistry, and English. They sometimes help build classrooms and science laboratories and design lessons for newer areas of education, such as HIV/AIDS education and environmental issues. Peace Corps volunteers in Kenya have also been working to help communities adopt farming practices that reduce soil erosion and slow down the clearing of forests.

Development Agencies

The United States and Canada have played key roles in the United Nations since its establishment in 1945 as an international organization that promotes world peace and economic cooperation. More than a dozen U.N. agencies operate in Kenya, bringing together many people from the United States, Canada, and other nations to work toward improving health, health care, and living conditions. Nairobi is the international headquarters for the U.N. Environment Program (UNEP). Established in 1946, the United Nations Children's Fund (UNICEF) aims to improve children's welfare, especially in developing and wartorn countries. UNICEF programs have brought many North Americans to Kenya, including celebrity UNICEF ambassadors, such as the late Audrey Hepburn. North American nongovernmental organizations, such as the Canadian Organization for Development Through Education, also work on health, educational, environmental, human rights, and other development projects in Kenya.

NAIROBI: INTERNATIONAL CENTER

Close to one hundred countries are represented in Nairobi, and Kenya has more diplomatic representation worldwide than any other sub-Saharan African country. Nairobi is also an important center for the World Bank, the United Nations, and international news agencies.

Left: **Audrey Hepburn visited northern Kenya as a UNICEF ambassador in 1992.**

Above: **Kenyan band African Heritage performs in Nairobi. American and Kenyan musicians have given joint concerts and performances in both countries.**

Music

Like many African countries, Kenya's influence in North America has been subtle. Many American music styles, especially the rhythms of blues and jazz, bear African musical influences. Today, musicians from Kenya and the United States collaborate and share styles. Members of the Saifee Band, which originated in Mombasa, Kenya, have performed with American musicians in Texas.

Film

The Kenyan savanna and its animals have inspired American films. Hollywood celebrities Meryl Streep and Robert Redford starred in the award-winning film *Out of Africa*, a portrayal of the lives of Kenya's European settlers in the 1920s and 1930s. The film was based on a novel of the same title, by Danish writer Isak Dinesen. More recently, the animated film and Broadway show *The Lion King* feature the animals of East Africa. Many of the characters' names are derived from Swahili words.

Kenyan Art

Most tribal art is ceremonial or ornamental in origin and traditionally played a part in daily life. The Maasai, for instance, decorate their spears and shields, and the Kisii decorate sitting stools. While this type of art is still common, many artists today also work for commercial reasons and cater to markets at home and overseas.

A variety of Kenyan products and handicrafts are popular with North Americans. These include sisal baskets and Kamba wood carvings. Overseas demand for these goods affected the development of art forms and techniques in Kenya. The Kamba have always made wooden stools, but they did not begin carving wood for sale until after World War I. Kamba woodcarver Mutisia Munge learned his art from the Zaramo people in Tanzania and brought these skills back to his people in Kenya. Many carving centers have developed in Kenya to meet demand for wooden figurines and ornaments. Some carvers even work on assembly-line production. Most Kamba carvings are of animals, human figures, masks, and utensils, such as bowls, spoons, salad forks, and napkin rings.

***Left:* A Kamba carver displays his creations, figures from African myths. Although they use many kinds of wood, the Kamba usually carve from rosewood or African blackwood (ebony).**

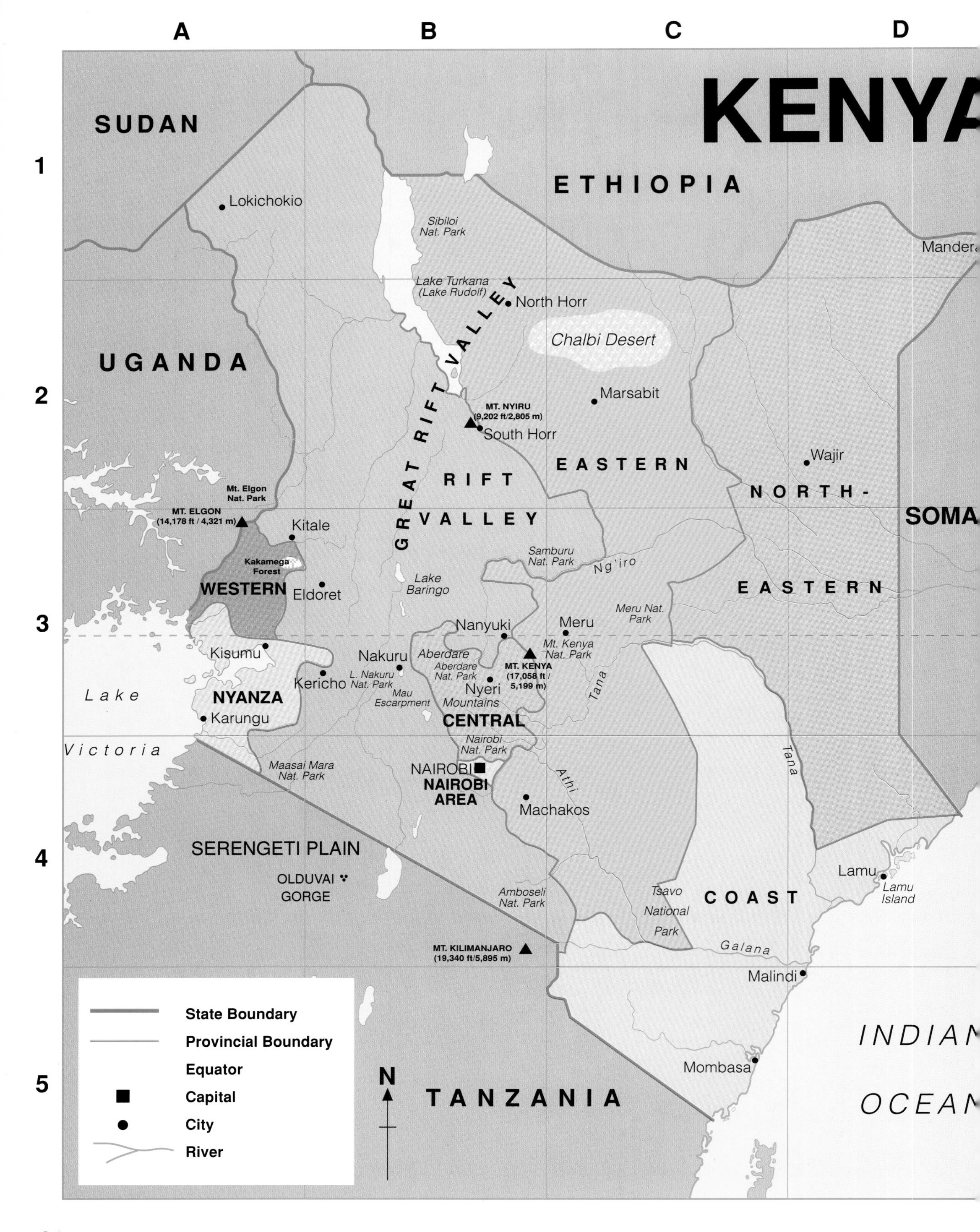
A
B
C
D
1
2
3
4
5
KENYA
SUDAN
ETHIOPIA
UGANDA
Lokichokio
Sibiloi Nat. Park
Lake Turkana (Lake Rudolf)
North Horr
Chalbi Desert
Mandera
GREAT RIFT VALLEY
Marsabit
MT. NYIRU (9,202 ft/2,805 m)
South Horr
EASTERN
Wajir
RIFT VALLEY
NORTH-EASTERN
SOMA
Mt. Elgon Nat. Park
MT. ELGON (14,178 ft / 4,321 m)
Kitale
Kakamega Forest
WESTERN
Eldoret
Lake Baringo
Samburu Nat. Park
Ng'iro
Meru Nat. Park
Nanyuki
Meru
Mt. Kenya Nat. Park
MT. KENYA (17,058 ft / 5,199 m)
Kisumu
Nakuru
Aberdare
Aberdare Nat. Park
L. Nakuru Nat. Park
Kericho
Nyeri
Mau Escarpment
Mountains
Tana
Lake Victoria
NYANZA
Karungu
CENTRAL
Nairobi Nat. Park
Maasai Mara Nat. Park
NAIROBI
NAIROBI AREA
Athi
Machakos
SERENGETI PLAIN
OLDUVAI GORGE
Amboseli Nat. Park
Tsavo National Park
COAST
Lamu
Lamu Island
Galana
MT. KILIMANJARO (19,340 ft/5,895 m)
Malindi
State Boundary
Provincial Boundary
Equator
Capital
City
River
N
TANZANIA
INDIAN OCEAN
Mombasa

Above: **A waterhole in Tsavo West National Park attracts many kinds of animals, including antelope.**

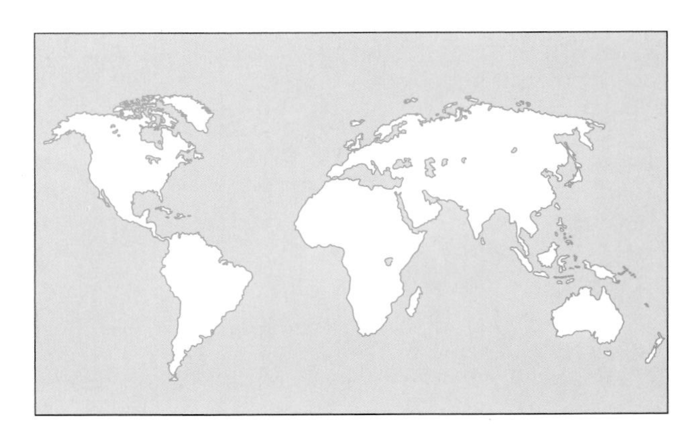

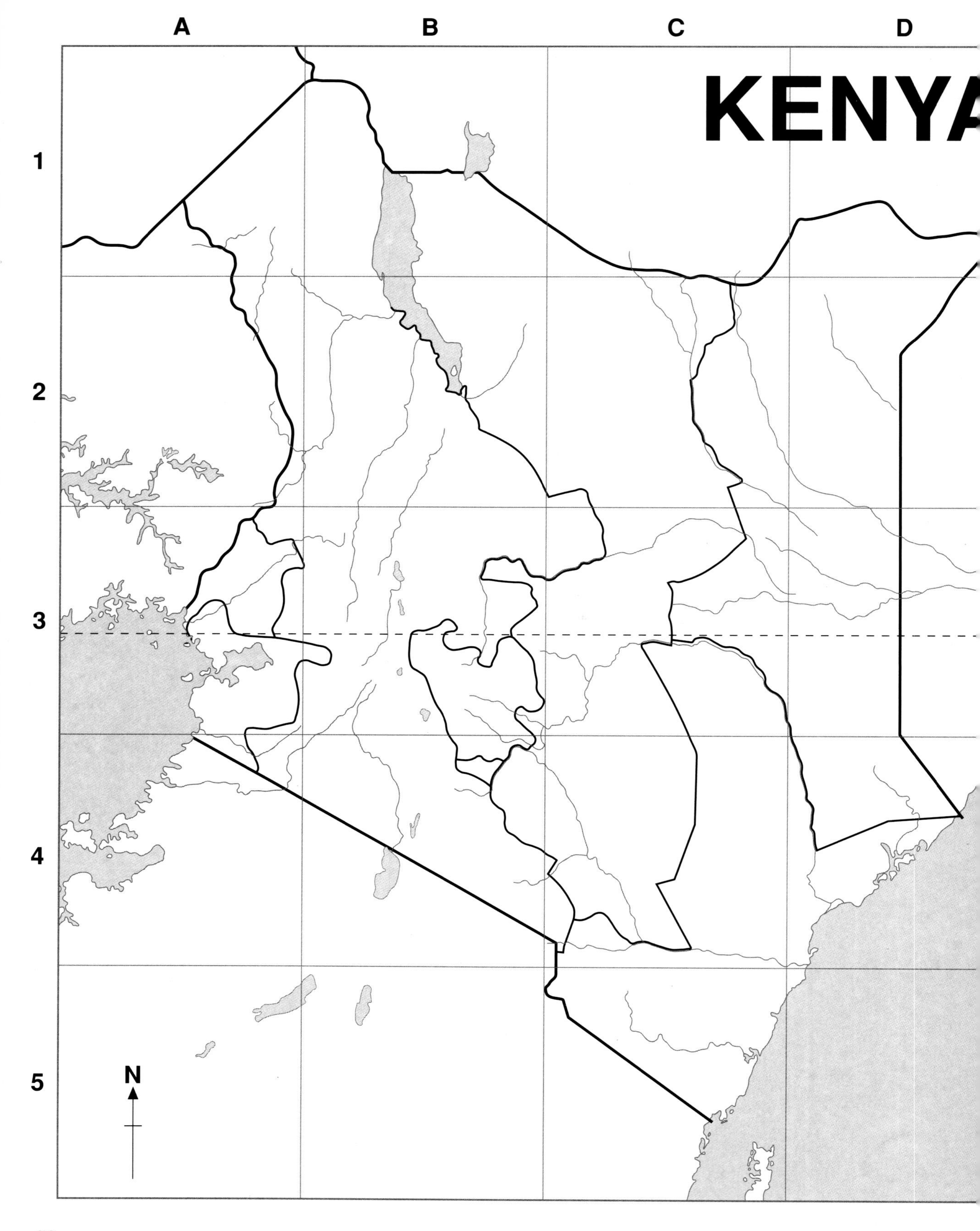
KENYA
A
B
C
D
1
2
3
4
5
N

How Is Your Geography?

Learning to identify the main geographical areas and points of a country can be challenging. Although it may seem difficult at first to memorize the locations and spellings of major cities or the names of mountain ranges, rivers, deserts, lakes, and other prominent physical features, the end result of this effort can be very rewarding. Places you previously did not know existed will suddenly come to life when referred to in world news, whether in newspapers, television reports, or other books and reference sources. This knowledge will make you feel a bit closer to the rest of the world, with its fascinating variety of cultures and physical geography.

Used in a classroom setting, the instructor can make duplicates of this map using a copy machine. (PLEASE DO NOT WRITE IN THIS BOOK!) Students can then fill in any requested information on their individual map copies. Used one-on-one, the student can also make copies of the map on a copy machine and use them as a study tool. The student can practice identifying place names and geographical features on his or her own.

Below: **Pelicans are among the many wetland birds of Lake Nakuru.**

Kenya at a Glance

Official Name	Republic of Kenya, or *Jamhuri Ya Kenya*
Capital	Nairobi
Official Language	English
National Language	Swahili
Population	28,241,000 (1998 estimate)
Land Area	224,961 square miles (582,801 square km)
Provinces	Central, Coast, Eastern, Nairobi Area, North-Eastern, Nyanza, Rift Valley, Western
Highest Point	Mt. Kenya (17,058 ft/5,199 m)
Major River	Tana River
Main Tribes	Kalenjin, Kamba, Kikuyu, Luhya, Luo
Literacy Rate	79 percent (86 percent for men, 70 percent for women, 1995 estimate)
Famous Leaders	Jomo Kenyatta (c. 1894–1978); Wangari Maathai (1940–); Thomas Mboya (1930–1969); Daniel arap Moi (1924–); Oginga Odinga (c. 1911–1994)
Major Cities	Kisumu, Mombasa, Nairobi, Nakuru
Major Festivals	Moi Day (October 10)
	Kenyatta Day (October 20)
	Jamhuri/Independence Day (December 12)
Major Exports	coffee, tea, sisal, pyrethrum, petroleum products, cotton, flowering plants
Major Imports	machinery, fertilizers, crude petroleum, chemicals and pharmaceuticals, manufactured goods
Currency	Kenyan shilling (61.39 Ksh = U.S. $1 as of 1999)

Opposite: **Nairobi boasts many modern office buildings.**

Glossary

African Vocabulary

asante (ah-SAN-tay): thank you.

benga (BAIN-gah): a musical style of the Luo people also adopted by Kikuyu and Kamba people.

chai (CHAY-ee): afternoon tea served with milk and sugar.

duka (DOO-kah): small shops usually run by Indian or Pakistani families who have settled in Nairobi and elsewhere in Kenya.

egekobo (EY-gay-ko-bo): escort; one of the Kisii marriage ceremonies.

erokenya (ARR-oh-KEN-yah): snow; along with *Kirinyaga*, possibly the origin of Kenya's current name.

harambee (ha-rahm-BAY): pulling together; a post-independence political term coined by Jomo Kenyatta to urge Kenya's diverse ethnic groups to unite.

isukhuti (EE-soo-koo-tee): a traditional drumming style practiced by the Luhya.

jambo (JAHM-bo): hello.

Jamhuri ya Kenya (JAHM-hur-i YAH KENYA): the Republic of Kenya, the country's official name.

kigogo (ki-GO-go): a simple, popular game of strategy that involves moving counters around a board to capture the opponent's pieces.

Kirinyaga (KER-ray-NYAH-gah): Mountain of Whiteness; along with *erokenya*, possibly the origin of Kenya's current name.

lorora (lor-OR-a): the circumcision ceremony for Samburu boys.

Maa (mah): the language shared by the Maasai and Samburu.

magadi (mah-GAH-dee): the alkaline lakes of the Great Rift Valley.

manyatta (mahn-YAH-tah): a housing settlement of Maasai warriors.

moran (mor-AHN): a warrior.

mugoiyo (MOOG-oi-yoh): a Kikuyu dance after the long rains.

N'erobi (n-ay-ROB-ee): place of cold waters; what the Maasai called Nairobi before it became the capital of Kenya.

Ngai (en-GAI): the divine spirit of many Kenyan ethnic groups.

oloiboni (ol-oi-BON-ee): Maasai ritual leaders, believed to be reincarnated as snakes.

omutibo (om-ut-EE-bo): a Luhya musical style that is a combination of guitar music and tapping on soda bottles.

rukiu (ROO-kee-oo): a basic dance of the Kikuyu that imparts steps and rhythms useful for later dances.

rumba (room-BAH): a popular Kenyan musical style characterized by complex rhythms.

safari (sah-far-EE): a journey; an expedition for hunting, exploration, or photography, especially in East Africa. Kenya's safari parks now prohibit hunting.

tarabu (tahr-ah-BOO): a Swahili musical style popular along the coast of Kenya.

ugali (OO-gahl-ee): a semisolid cornmeal porridge served with vegetables or meat.

English Vocabulary

acacia: a thorny, flat-topped family of trees commonly found in the savanna.

alleged: declared; stated.

aphrodisiac: a food, drug, or other substance that arouses or is reputed to arouse sexual desire.

Bantu: one of the three major language and ethnic groups in Kenya. Bantu groups include the Kamba, Kikuyu, Kisii, Luhya, and Meru peoples.

capitalistic: describing an economic system in which wealth is made and maintained by private individuals or corporations.

circumcision: the act of removing the fold of skin covering the male or female sexual organ, especially as a ceremonial or religious rite.

constitution: the system of principles according to which a nation is governed.

coup d'etat: unexpected political uprising.

Cushite: one of the three major language and ethnic groups in Kenya. Cushitic groups include the Boran, Oromo, Rendille, and Somali peoples.

dhow: a sailing vessel used by Arabs.

incentive: something that incites action or greater effort.

initiation: the ceremonies or rites of acceptance into a certain group.

market economy: an economy in which prices are freely determined by the activity of buyers and sellers.

Mau Mau: a militant nationalist movement, made up mainly of Kikuyu, opposed to British rule in Kenya in the 1950s.

Nilote: one of the three major language and ethnic groups in Kenya. Nilotic groups include the Kalenjin, Luo, Maasai, Samburu, and Turkana.

nomadic: describing a person or group that moves from place to place in search of food or pasture.

perpetuating: preserving; continuing.

placard: sign.

plantains: tropical plants belonging to the banana family.

polygamy: as practiced by many African tribes, the act of having more than one wife.

protectorate: a state or territory under the protection and partial control of another state, power, or country.

pyrethrum: a kind of chrysanthemum with finely divided leaves and red, pink, lilac, or white flowers. Dried pyrethrum can be used as an insecticide or as a cure for certain skin disorders.

savanna: dry grassland with thorny scrub.

sisal: a fiber produced by the agave plant.

soda ash: a grayish white sodium salt.

squatters: native Kenyans whose land was taken during British colonial rule and who remained on parcels of their land in return for labor or rent.

totem: an animal or plant used to represent a clan, family group, or tribe.

tribe: a group of people who share a common ethnic identity, ancestry, language, and customs.

unicameral: describing a legislative body that consists of a single chamber or house.

urban peasants: the name given to Nairobi's landless, homeless people.

More Books to Read

An African Experience: Wildlife, Art, and Adventure in Kenya. Simon Combes (Greenwich)

African Warriors: The Samburu. Thomasin Magor (Harry N. Abrams)

Animals of Africa. Thomas B. Allen (Levine Associates)

Being Oromo in Kenya. Mario I. Aguilar (Red Sea)

The Cats of Lamu. Jack Couffer (Lyons Press)

Kenya. Dalvan M. Coger (Clio Press)

Kenya: Africa's Tamed Wilderness. Discovering Our Heritage series. Joann Johansen Burch (Dillon)

Kenya's Changing Landscape. R. M. Turner (University of Arizona Press)

Our Life: A View of Maasai Women. (Centre of Biodiversity of the National Museums of Kenya)

Safari: Journey to the End. J. David Taylor (Boston Mills)

Thomas Joseph Mboya: A Biography. Edwin Gimonde (East African Edition Publishers)

The Wisdom of the Bones: In Search of Human Origins. Alan Walker and Pat Shipman (Knopf)

Videos

Reflections on Elephants. (National Geographic Society)

Wings Over the Serengeti. (National Geographic Society)

Web Sites

www.africaonline.com

www.kenyaweb.com

www.kenyanamerican.com

www.peacecorps.gov/www/dp/ww1.html

Due to the dynamic nature of the Internet, some web sites stay current longer than others. To find additional web sites, use a reliable search engine with one or more of the following keywords to help you locate information about Kenya. Keywords: *East Africa, Great Rift Valley, Kenyan, Richard Leakey, Maasai, Daniel arap Moi, Nairobi, safari.*

Index

DATE DUE
